高职高专院校专业基础课纸数融合系列教材

供临床医学、口腔医学、护理、助产、药学、影像、检验等专业使用

高职基础英语

GAOZHI JICHU YINGYU

主　编　江晓东　邬文婷　余仕湖
副主编　周德纯　谢家鑫　曾静华　庞　凌
编　者　（以姓氏笔画为序）
　　　　邬文婷　江晓东　吴丹迪　余仕湖
　　　　周德纯　庞　凌　曾静华　谢家鑫

华中科技大学出版社
http://www.hustp.com
中国·武汉

内 容 简 介

本书为高职高专院校专业基础课纸数融合系列教材。

本书参考高等学校英语应用能力考试大纲,针对高职高专学生的需求和学力基础等具体情况,充分利用二语习得的相关理论进行编写。全书共分为10个单元,每个单元围绕一个特定的主题(大学、音乐、健康、运动等)编写,每一主题都贴近学生的学习、生活。此外,本书选材注重知识性、实用性、时代性、趣味性,在注重语言能力提升的同时,也兼顾语言学习的通识教育,有助于提高学生的文化素养。

本书可供高职专科、成人专科学生学习,亦可供具有一定英语基础知识的社会人员自主学习。

图书在版编目(CIP)数据

高职基础英语/江晓东,邬文婷,余仕湖主编.—武汉:华中科技大学出版社,2020.8(2021.8 重印)
ISBN 978-7-5680-6483-5

Ⅰ.①高…　Ⅱ.①江…　②邬…　③余…　Ⅲ.①英语-高等职业教育-教材　Ⅳ.①H319.39

中国版本图书馆 CIP 数据核字(2020)第 149652 号

高职基础英语　　　　　　　　　　　　　　江晓东　邬文婷　余仕湖　主编
Gaozhi Jichu Yingyu

策划编辑：居　颖
责任编辑：曾奇峰
封面设计：原色设计
责任校对：曾　婷
责任监印：周治超
出版发行：华中科技大学出版社(中国·武汉)　　电话：(027)81321913
　　　　　武汉市东湖新技术开发区华工科技园　　邮编：430223
录　　排：华中科技大学惠友文印中心
印　　刷：武汉科源印刷设计有限公司
开　　本：889mm×1194mm　1/16
印　　张：9.5
字　　数：289 千字
版　　次：2021 年 8 月第 1 版第 2 次印刷
定　　价：49.80 元

本书若有印装质量问题,请向出版社营销中心调换
全国免费服务热线：400-6679-118　　竭诚为您服务
版权所有　侵权必究

网络增值服务使用说明

欢迎使用华中科技大学出版社医学资源网 yixue.hustp.com

1. 教师使用流程

   （1）登录网址：http://yixue.hustp.com （注册时请选择教师用户）

   注册 → 登录 → 完善个人信息 → 等待审核

   （2）审核通过后，您可以在网站使用以下功能：

   教师：建立课程、管理学生、布置作业、下载教学资源、查询学生学习记录等

2. 学员使用流程

   建议学员在PC端完成注册、登录、完善个人信息的操作。

   （1）PC端学员操作步骤

   ① 登录网址：http://yixue.hustp.com （注册时请选择普通用户）

   注册 → 登录 → 完善个人信息

   ② 查看课程资源

   如有学习码，请在个人中心-学习码验证中先验证，再进行操作。

   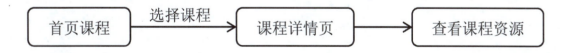

   首页课程 —选择课程→ 课程详情页 → 查看课程资源

   （2）手机端扫码操作步骤

   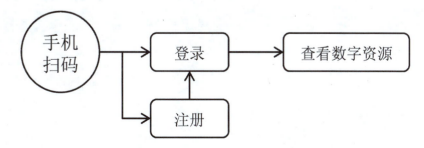

Preface 前 言

  本书根据教育部高等教育司颁布的《高职高专教育英语课程教学基本要求(试行)》的相关内容,参考高等学校英语应用能力考试大纲,针对高职高专学生的具体情况,充分利用二语习得的相关理论进行编写。本书旨在提高学生听、说、读、写、译各个层面的语言应用能力,通过丰富合理的选材强化学生在上述各方面的语言输出能力,充分体现了以"学生为中心"的教学理念。

  在本书的编写过程中,编者查阅了大量的资料,了解了当前高等职业院校公共外语教材编写的先进理念和方法,为编写工作提供了科学的指导。编者力图在本书的编写过程中,根据高职高专学生的英语基础能力的现状和学习心理特点,以各种语言习得的相关理论为指导,把英语教学的新模式与英语教学的新理论、新进展、新观念有机整合,侧重选材的新颖性与信息性,注重实用性和时代性,强化以学生发展为本的理念,以适应课堂任务型教学,并注重学生自主学习能力的培养。

  本书共 10 个单元。每个单元涉及一个常见的与生活或学习相关的主题,由 Look and Learn、Speak and Learn、Read and Learn、Practice and Learn 以及 Write and Learn 五个部分组成。Look and Learn 为话题导入和探索部分,提供与主题相关的单词及对应的图片,使学生熟悉主题并引导学生积极参与话题的讨论。Speak and Learn 为听说部分,提供与单元主题紧密相关的对话,旨在提高学生的听力能力,同时学生能通过对话内容的学习逐步提高口语表达能力。Read and Learn 为阅读部分,含与主题相关的两篇阅读文章,重点提升学生的英语阅读能力并开阔学生的视野;此外,每篇文章后相应的练习题进一步强化学生对课文知识的理解和应用。Practice and Learn 为语法部分,该部分涵盖英语中的部分重点语法知识,旨在加强巩固学生的语法知识。Write and Learn 为写作部分,内容主要涉及常见的应用文写作,如病假条、留言条、申请表等,旨在帮助学生理解和掌握各种应用文的写作方法和技巧。

  本书由重庆三峡医药高等专科学校部分英语教师编写。其中,第一单元、第五单元、第十单元以及 Glossary 部分由江晓东负责编写;第二单元由周德纯负责编写;第三单元由谢家鑫负责编写;第四单元由曾静华负责编写;第六单元由庞凌负责编写;第七单元由余仕湖负责编写;第八单元由吴丹迪负责编写;第九单元由邬文婷负责编写。

  在本书编写过程中,校内外的许多同事和学生提供了帮助。重庆三峡学院的刘晓林教授、重庆医药高等专科学校的王炎峰副教授、重庆医科大学的陈琰晗副教授对本书编写工作提出了很多中肯的宝贵建议;重庆医科大学向艳萍同学和南京师范大学江禾同学花了大量时间参与材料初选、文本试读、生词核对、文字处理、初稿打印等基础但耗时的工作。本书编写组对以上教师和学生表示衷心的感谢。本书课文选材时,编者参阅了大量网上和报刊资料,同时也从其他同类书籍中得到了很多借鉴和启发,在此向相关作者和编者表示衷心感谢。

  鉴于编者能力有限,书中可能还存在错漏之处,敬请本书使用者批评指正。

编 者

目 录
MULU

Unit 1	College	1
Unit 2	Music	11
Unit 3	Health	21
Unit 4	Food	31
Unit 5	Family	42
Unit 6	Sports	53
Unit 7	Travel	64
Unit 8	Shopping	76
Unit 9	Psychology	87
Unit 10	Life	98

练习参考答案　　　　　　　　　　　　　　　　　　　　109

参考译文　　　　　　　　　　　　　　　　　　　　　　118

Glossary　　　　　　　　　　　　　　　　　　　　　　129

Unit 1   College

Learning Objectives:

To *describe* your campus and your college life in English.
To *improve* the reading skills like scanning for main ideas and details in the texts.
To *adapt* yourself to the changes and challenges in your new college life.
To *understand* the grammar rules related to English word formation.
To *learn to write* an invitation letter in English.

Part 1   Look and Learn

Warming-up: Look at the following pictures, talk about them and then finish Task 1

classroom

cafeteria

dorm

library

lab

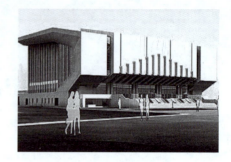
gym

New Words

classroom [ˈklɑːsrʊm] n. a room in a school where lessons take place 教室

cafeteria [ˌkæfɪˈtɪərɪə] n. a restaurant where you choose and pay for your meal at a counter and carry it to a table 自助餐厅

dorm [dɔːm] n. a room for several people to sleep in, especially in a school or other institutions 集体宿舍, 学生宿舍

library [ˈlaɪbrərɪ] n. a building in which collections of books, CDs, newspapers, etc. are kept for people to read, study or borrow 图书馆

lab [læb] n. a room or building used for scientific research, experiments, testing, etc. 实验室

gym [dʒɪm] n. a room or hall with equipment for doing physical exercises, for example in a school 体育馆

Task 1 Match the words in the left column with the explanations in the right column

1. major	A. a student who has already received one degree and is studying at a university for a more advanced degree
2. diploma	B. the most important subject that a college student is studying
3. bachelor's degree	C. a document given by a college to show that you have passed a particular exam or finished your study
4. undergraduate	D. the first degree at a college or university
5. postgraduate	E. a student who is studying for the first degree at a college or university

Part 2 Speak and Learn

Task 2 Complete the conversation with the following expressions

A. a wide variety
B. On the first floor
C. a friendly campus tour guide
D. attend our lectures
E. enjoy new activities

Steve: Hi, Emily. Congratulations on being a college student. I am so glad to show you around the campus.

Emily: Thank you, Steve. You are so nice and helpful. I am sure I will be 1. _____ just like you for the freshmen this time next year.

Steve: Let me first show you the way to the students' cafeteria. It is just in front of the students' apartments. You can't miss it.

Emily: What kind of food does it offer? When is it open?

Steve: It provides 2. _____ of food choices from 6:00 a.m. to 10:00 p.m.

Emily: That sounds good.

Steve: Okay, our next stop is the teaching building. Look at that building with seven floors. We 3. _____ there every day.

Emily: How tall the building is! The multi-media classrooms are so spacious.

Steve: This is the shortcut to the college library, where you can see a large collection of paper books, electronic books, newspapers and magazines.

Emily: What is the first floor of the library for?

Steve: 4. _____, there are some rooms for reading, self-study and group discussion. Our last stop is the students' recreational center. Some clubs are recruiting freshmen.

Emily: What club can I join on campus?

Steve: We have an English association, a debate team, a cartoon club, and different sports clubs, just to name a few.

Emily: Sounds awesome.

Steve: My tips for you are to 5. _____ and meet new people.

Emily: I would be only too happy to. Thank you for your advice.

Task 3 Answer the following questions according to the dialogue in no more than 3 words

1. What does Steve offer to help Emily?
   He _____ the campus and offers to be her college tour guide.
2. Which place do they visit first?
   Their first stop is the _____.
3. How large are the multi-media classrooms in the teaching building?
   The multi-media classrooms in the teaching building are _____.
4. Where can you go for your self-study and group discussion on campus?
   We can do that on the _____ of the library.
5. Which group can Emily join if she likes English learning?
   She can join _____.

Task 4 Discuss with your partners about the benefits and drawbacks of living independently with the help of the following expressions

In high school

1. You can count on your parents and your teachers to remind you of your duties and responsibilities.

2. When you are confused about making decisions, your father and mother will always there to help you set priorities.

3. When you stay home, your parents arrange most things, including laundry.

In college

1. You have to manage your time so as not to fail in your exams.

2. The college students are supposed to be more initiative in whatever they should do.

3. You have to learn how to get along with your roommates. Some of them even have behaviors and habits different from you.

Part 3　Read and Learn

Passage A

Homesickness in College Life

College is supposed to be the best time in your life. Often, this is true for many people, as they get to enjoy newfound freedom away from their parents or **guardians**, meeting new friends, and experiencing new fun things. However, one aspect of going to college that many people don't talk about is homesickness. Below are practical ways to deal with homesickness in college life.

First, living away from home doesn't mean that you have to struggle with **adjusting to** a new environment. To make it easier on you, bring some home comforts to your dorm room. Often, a family photo, **souvenirs**, and bedding **have tremendous impacts on** how welcome you will feel anytime you step in your dorm room.

Second, try to be **sociable**. As tempting as it may be, sitting in your dorm room and thinking about how much you miss home will only make your homesickness worse. One way of dealing with this is to get out and meet new people. Meeting new people allows you to find new friends with whom you will share home life experiences without being **saddened** by them.

Last but not least, look after yourself. Avoid the **temptation** of sleeping and **excessively** eating all day. Instead, choose to get **sufficient** sleep but not to the point that you are in a **depressive** state. Additionally, choose to eat healthy balanced meal **portions** and schedule a time for exercise for a release of feel good **hormones**.

As seen above, homesickness is perfectly normal for many people. Give yourself **ample** time to adjust and **purposefully** keep yourself busy. Above all, don't be ashamed of homesickness. You will **quell** your anxiety and **minimize** your feeling of homesickness.

New Words

guardian [ˈɡɑːdɪən] n. a person who is legally responsible for the care of another person, especially a child whose parents have died 监护人

souvenir [ˌsuːvəˈnɪər] n. a thing that you buy and/or keep to remind yourself of a place, an occasion or a holiday/vacation 纪念品, 纪念物

sociable [ˈsəʊʃəbl] adj. enjoying spending time with other people 好交际的, 合群的

sadden [ˈsædn] v. to make someone sad 使悲伤, 使伤心

temptation [tempˈteɪʃn] n. the desire to do or have something that you know is bad or wrong 引诱, 诱惑

excessively [ɪkˈsesɪvli] adv. to a degree exceeding normal or proper limits 过分地, 极度地

sufficient [səˈfɪʃnt] adj. enough for a particular purpose; as much as you need 足够的, 充足的

depressive [dɪˈpresɪv] adj. connected with the medical condition of depression 抑郁的

portion [ˈpɔːʃn] n. an amount of food that is large enough for a person （食物）一份

hormone [ˈhɔːməʊn] n. a chemical substance produced in the body or in a plant that encourages growth or influences how the cells and tissues function 激素

ample [ˈæmpl] adj. enough or more than enough 足够的, 丰裕的

purposefully [ˈpɜːpəsfʊli] adv. in a purposeful manner 有意地

minimize [ˈmɪnɪmaɪz] v. to reduce something especially something bad to the lowest possible level 使减少到最低限度

Phrases

adjust to 调整

have tremendous impacts on 对……产生巨大影响

quell one's anxiety 消除某人的焦虑

Task 5 Fill in the blanks with the words given below and change the word forms if necessary

1. Some high school students just can't wait to enjoy their _____(free) away from home.

2. You have to overcome your _____(homesick) when you miss your father and mother in a distant place.

3. The overseas students are struggling with _____(adjust) themselves to a new environment.

4. Could you tell me on which floor of this department store I can buy some clothes and _____(bed) like blankets and pillows.

5. Mary is quite _____(society) and she feels easy to get along with strangers in new places.

6. Somebody says that human beings can resist anything but _____(tempt) excessively.

7. The patient has been suffering from mild _____(depress) for more than ten years.

8. I had no intention of breaking your cup into pieces. I didn't do it _____(purpose).

9. As medical professionals, we have to _____(minimum) the risk of this operation.

10. The news that the well-known scientist died really _____(sad) me last week.

Task 6 Choose the correct answer according to the passage

1. What is the main idea of this passage? _____

A. College students find it very easy to adjust to the new environment in their college

B. Bringing some home comforts to your college apartments is a fantastic idea

C. Some practical ways are available to handle homesickness in college life

D. Meeting new friends and experiencing fun things can be possible for every student

2. What is not mentioned in the passage as a home comfort to bring to your college? _____

  A. souvenir   B. bedding   C. a family photo   D. mother's dish

3. Why does being sociable help college students overcome their homesickness according to this passage? _____

  A. Making friends will worsen your feeling of homesickness

  B. You can sit in your dorm room and write a letter to your friends

  C. You can communicate with your friends, sharing home life experiences with them

  D. Your friends can not sadden you because you are strong

4. What does the word "sufficient" in the last but one paragraph mean in English? _____

  A. effective   B. efficient   C. suffering   D. enough

5. Which of the following is implied in the last paragraph? _____

  A. It is natural that every freshman in college may feel homesick to some extent

  B. Keeping doing things all the time will be not good for you

  C. Some students do not have enough time to adjust themselves to the new environment

  D. Eating healthy and balanced meal is an effective way to quell your homesickness

Task 7 Translate the following sentences into Chinese

1. The popularization of electronic products such as mobile phones, computers and tablets has a tremendous impact on the cognitive and intellectual development of students.

_____

2. You should get sufficient rest but not to the point that you feel dull and boring.

_____

3. One way of dealing with air pollution is to reduce carbon emission by stopping overusing cars.

_____

4. He is someone who would like to take on challenges and adjust to a new environment wherever he is.

_____

5. One aspect of learning English that many people ignore is linguistic skills such as listening and speaking.

_____

Passage B

Dealing with Feeling Lost

When I arrived at college, I expected everything to quickly fall into place. I'd be that girl in the movies who started off shy and nervous, but then found her club or her friends and had the world at her **fingertips**.

Because college is not like the movies, this don't happen. I saw that the girls on my floor become best friends while my roommates and I were only **amicable with** each other. I remember that I was **jealous of** a floor mate — not because she had a full **scholarship**, but because upon arriving at college she immediately had a group to **bond with**.

Surrounded by 15,000 other students, I felt lost. I couldn't **comprehend** how everyone else was having such an easy time adjusting to college. They all seemed to have found their place and by

sophomore year when I still hadn't. I felt that it was already too late for me.

I realized that I had to put myself out there if I wanted new experiences. I went on a surfing trip with the school's outdoor adventure club, and I joined a volunteer club where I **mentored** a fifth grade girl. Each time I took a chance on something new, it was scary, but I had a feeling that it would be worth it. I was meeting new people, trying new things, and **expanding** my comfort zone. As college went on I became more confident in myself. Some of my efforts failed, but other things shaped my college experience and now my career.

As a freshman, feeling lost at college felt like the end of the world. Looking back, I'm glad that I went through that period. It's natural to feel lost in college and I have realized that everyone feels it to some extent. College is a time of **transition** in life, but feeling uncertain shouldn't be used as an excuse to stand still and not try new things. People should **embrace** feeling lost and use it as an opportunity to explore anything they want.

I could have spent all four years cooped up in my dorm room wondering why nothing changed, but instead I got up, **immersed** myself **in** campus life, and became better for it. Feeling lost made me push myself. It took some time, but instead of letting it defeat me, I let it open me up.

New Words

fingertip ['fɪŋgərtɪp] n. the end of the finger that is the furthest from the hand 指尖

scholarship ['skɒləʃɪp] n. an amount of money given to somebody by an organization to help pay for his or her education 奖学金

surround [sə'raʊnd] v. to be all around something or somebody 围绕，环绕

comprehend [ˌkɒmprɪ'hend] v. to understand something fully 理解，领悟

sophomore ['sɒfəmɔːr] n. a student in the second year of a college or university（大学）二年级学生

mentor ['mentɔːr] v. to give someone help and advice over a period of time, especially help and advice related to their job 指导，辅导

expand [ɪk'spænd] v. become larger in size or volume or quantity 扩大，增加

transition [træn'zɪʃn] n. the process or a period of changing from one state or condition to another 过渡，变迁，转变

embrace [ɪm'breɪs] v. to accept an idea, a proposal, a set of beliefs, etc., especially when it is done with enthusiasm 欣然接受，乐意采纳

Phrases

be amicable with 与……友好相处
be jealous of 嫉妒……
bond with 结合
immerse in 沉浸在……

Task 8 Fill in the blanks with the words given below and change the word forms if necessary

1. I feel _____ (jealousy) of what you have achieved in your English learning.

2. It is not easy to obtain a full _____ (scholar) from that top university since it has lots of requirements.

3. Our beautiful campus is located beside a river and _____ (surrounding) by some gorgeous hills.

4. In many English tests, reading _____ (comprehend) part needs you to read three or four passages and finish some exercises in a limited time.

5. It was an _____ (adventure) field trip but my friends and I enjoyed it so much.

6. The barking dog _____ (scary) the toddler and he began to cry for help.

7. The country _____ (expansion) its territory southward in the 18th century.

8. As a freshman, building _____ (confident) is the first step to start you new college life.

9. It's _____ (nature) for us to feel nervous and stressful when we are in a new environment.

10. I had a sense of _____ (uncertain) when my friend asked me what I was going to be in the future because I was still unsure of my career path at time.

Task 9 Choose the correct answer according to the passage

1. What is true for the writer according to the passage? _____
A. She had a high expectation of her quick adjustment to the new college life
B. She thought that college life was like a movie, full of fun and stories
C. She felt too shy and nervous to find her club and her friends
D. She made a lot of friends in her dorm as soon as she arrived

2. What do we call a second-year college student? _____
A. freshman   B. sophomore   C. junior   D. senior

3. Why did the writer become green-eyed with a floor mate? _____
A. Because the floor mate obtained a full scholarship
B. Because the floor mate was amicable with the writer
C. Because the floor mate got to college and made some friends very soon
D. Because the floor mate didn't have a sense of belonging and felt marginalized

4. How did the writer try to do to change and improve her college life? _____
A. She decided to stop being friendly to her roommates
B. She gained some scholarships to have a positive impact on her career
C. She felt lost and uncertain so she wanted to quit school
D. She started to try something new even if it frightened her a little bit at first

5. What did the writer feel when she looked back her whole college life? _____
A. She regretted doing nothing to challenge herself in those years
B. She felt that she made a right decision when she managed to step out of her comfort zone

C. She thought that campus life was temporary and she just waited and did nothing

D. She didn't push herself as a college student and she felt natural

Part 4 Practice and Learn

Word Formation（构词法）

常见的英语构词法有派生法、合成法、转化法、截短法、混合法和首字母缩略法。

1. 派生法

在词根前面加前缀或在词根后面加后缀,从而构成一个与原单词意义相近或截然相反的新词的方法叫派生法。

(1) 前缀:除少数英语前缀外,前缀一般改变单词的意义,不改变词性,如 atypical(非典型的)、abnormal(异常的)。

(2) 后缀:后缀通常会改变单词的词性,构成意义相近的其他词,如 strengthen(加强)、differentiate(鉴别)。少数后缀还会改变词义,变为与原来词义相反的新词,如 careless(粗心的)。

2. 合成法

将两个单词连在一起合成一个新词,前一个词修饰或限定后一个词,这种方法就是合成法,如 makeshift(临时应急用物)、outbreak(爆发)。

3. 转化法

将一种词性用作另一种词性而词形不变的方法叫转化法,有的名词可以作为动词,有的形容词可以作为副词或动词,如 face 和 book。

4. 截短法

将单词缩写,词义和词性保持不变的方法称为截短法,主要有截头、去尾、截头去尾等形式,如 telephone→phone、airplane→plane。

5. 混合法

将两个词混合或各取一部分紧缩形成一个新词,前半部分表属性,后半部分表主体。这样的英语构词法就是混合法,如 smog。

6. 首字母缩略法

用单词首字母组成一个新词的英语构词法叫首字母缩略法。这种方法形成的新词的读音主要有两种形式,即各字母分别读音,或作为一个单词读音,如 AIDS。

Task 10 Point out the word which is different from the other three words in terms of English word formation

1. A. online   B. unlike   C. expression   D. explanation
2. A. disagree   B. unfair   C. impossible   D. handwriting
3. A. manmade   B. enlarge   C. cooperate   D. rewrite
4. A. widen   B. outlook   C. beautify   D. realize
5. A. Chinese   B. golden   C. eastern   D. weekend
6. A. everywhere   B. however   C. beforehand   D. anything
7. A. mathematics   B. examination   C. icebox   D. kilogram
8. A. influenza→flu   B. refrigerator→fridge
   C. prescription→script   D. laboratory→lab
9. A. news broadcast→newscast   B. television broadcast→telecast

C. helicopter airport→heliport   D. west ward→westward

10. A. SARS   B. AIDS   C. lab   D. ICU

Part 5　Write and Learn

A Letter of Invitation（邀请函）

邀请函包括晚会、社团活动、宴会、舞会、晚餐、婚礼等各种活动的邀请信件。邀请函的写作要求叙事清楚、明白，涉及的人物、时间、地点要表达无误。一般而言，写邀请函时应该包括以下内容：简要说明活动并邀请对方；参加活动的时间和地点；邀请对方参加活动的原因；期待对方接受邀请并表示感谢。以下是英文邀请函的常见表达。

1. invite somebody to do something

2. have fun/have a good time/enjoy

3. long for your coming

4. On behalf of all the students in the chemistry class, I am writing to invite you...

5. Here is a brief schedule about this meeting.

6. We sincerely hope you can accept our invitation.

7. Please let us know your decision if it is convenient for you.

【Sample】

假如你是经理John Smith，给公司员工Sara Brown写一封邀请函，代表你的团队邀请她参加2020年12月1日公司在希尔顿酒店举行的午宴，辞旧迎新。

Sara Brown,

On behalf of the entire team, I would like to invite you to a lunch party which the company is holding on December 1, 2020 at the Hilton Hotel.

This lunch party will be a celebration of finishing the year and moving on to new and exciting things within the company, and there's no better guest to invite than the man who makes sure everything in our great company runs smoothly.

We all hope that you will accept our invitation so that we can celebrate the success that our company has achieved and the prosperity that it will continue to achieve.

Respectfully yours,

John Smith, Manager

Task 11　Try to write a letter of invitation based on the information given below

假定你是李明，下个月你校将举办茶文化节。你想邀请英国朋友Jason来做一个英国茶文化的讲座，请写信告知，包括以下内容：简要介绍茶文化节活动；说明讲座主题是英国下午茶；询问下个星期五可否。注意：单词数一百左右；可以适当增加细节以使行文连贯。

Unit 2   Music

Learning Objectives:

To *describe* musical events in English.
To *cultivate* the learner's interest and hobby in music.
To *increase* the reading speed by skimming the passage.
To *understand* the grammar rules related to sentence constituents.
To *learn* to write an English note for sick leave.

Part 1   Look and Learn

Warming-up: Look at the following pictures, talk about them and then finish Task 1

stage

lyric

amplifier

instrument

backdrop

rhythm

New Words

stage [steɪdʒ] n. the structure for varieties of art performances 舞台

lyric [ˈlɪrɪk] n. the text of a song 歌词

amplifier [ˈæmplɪfaɪə] n. an electronic equipment to strengthen signals 扩音器，放大器

instrument [ˈɪnstrəmənt] n. a musical device that requires skill for proper use 乐器

backdrop [ˈbækdrɒp] n. scenery hung at the back of stage 背景

rhythm [ˈrɪð(ə)m] n. recurring at regular intervals in music 节奏

Task 1 Match the words in the left column with the explanations in the right column

1. volume	A. a long and complex sonata performed by orchestra
2. frequency	B. a drama set to music
3. symphony	C. any activity that is performed alone without assistance
4. solo	D. the number of occurrences in a given time
5. opera	E. the amount of sound

Part 2 Speak and Learn

Task 2 Complete the conversation with the following expressions

A. in memory of

B. which instruments will be played there

C. a symphony will be held on campus

D. The heated atmosphere

E. it is famous for its long history

Jenny: Are you a huge fan of music, Carl?

Carl: Definitely, Jenny. I am a sophomore majoring in classic music.

Jenny: That's terrific. Have you heard that 1. _____? Would you like to go with me?

Carl: I'd love to, but I wonder who will give the performance.

Jenny: Chicago Orchestra, one of the most leading 10 orchestras throughout the world and 2. _____.

Carl: That sounds exciting. By the way, would you mind telling me 3. _____?

Jenny: Oh, varieties of brass, keyboard as well as drum instruments.

4. _____ will impress you a great deal.

Carl: How awesome! Which song will be performed?

Jenny: *For Alice*. In 1810, the great German music giant, Beethoven, composed this piano solo 5. _____ the girl Alice he once loved deeply.

Carl: What a touching romantic story it was! When will the symphony be held?

Jenny: To be exact, 7:30 p.m. next Sunday. If you are willing to enjoy it along with me, we can get 2 tickets online and a discount will be offered.

Carl: Sure, just remember to remind me. I can't wait for it anymore and I am grateful for your help.

Jenny: You are welcome.

Task 3 Answer the following questions according to the dialogue in no more than 3 words

1. What does Carl major in?

   His major is _____.

2. Where will the symphony be held?

   It will be held _____.

3. Why has Chicago Orchestra become so popular in the world?

   It is famous for _____.

4. As for the symphony, what might most impress Jenny?

   _____ will definitely impress her deeply.

5. How much do you know about Beethoven?

   He was the great _____.

Task 4 Talk with your partners about a musical event with the help of the following expressions

1. I am a huge fan of pop music.
2. I am passionate/crazy about country music.
3. The concert/symphony/solo will be held in our school next week.
4. The percussion/string/keyboard instruments will be played.
5. The backdrop/scenery/sound effect/visual effect/light effect will be impressive.
6. The performers' costumes/expressions/actions will characterize the performance.

Part 3   Read and Learn

Passage A

Why Do We Love Music?

Music has been with us **as long as** we can collectively remember. Musical instruments have been found **dating back** to tens of thousands of years. Yet no one knows why we love music, or what function, if any, it serves.

Researchers have yet to find a "music center" in the brain. Like many higher-order processes, the tasks **involved** in processing and enjoying music are **distributed** across several brain areas.

One study found that when focusing on **harmony** in a piece, a subject experiences increased activity in the right **temporal lobe**'s **auditory** areas. Several studies have shown the temporal lobe to be

扫码听
课文A

Note

a key region for understanding certain musical **features**. But it works closely with areas in the frontal lobe **responsible for** forming meaningful musical structure.

Other studies have focused on our emotional responses to music. In 2001, an experiment at the McGill University used brain scans to study the **neural** mechanics of the **goose bumps** that great music can sometimes **induce**. They found that the brain structures **activated** are the same regions linked to other **stimuli**, such as food, sex and drugs. Blood flow in the brain rises and falls to swells of music in areas associated with reward, emotion and **arousal**.

As **stimulation** for food and sex is important for an **organism**'s **survival**, the fact that similar neural activity is observed in responses to features in music suggests that there could be some **evolutionary** advantages to the ability to hear or hum a good tune.

New Words

involve [ɪnˈvɒlv] v. to engage as a participant 包含,牵涉

distribute [dɪˈstrɪbjuːt] v. to spread widely 分布,散布

harmony [ˈhɑːməni] n. the state of constancy in opinion or action 和谐

auditory [ˈɔːdɪt(ə)ri] adj. relating to the process of hearing 听觉的

feature [ˈfiːtʃə] n. qualities or characteristics 特点,特征

neural [ˈnjʊərəl] adj. regarding the nervous system 神经的

induce [ɪnˈdjuːs] v. cause to arise 引诱

activate [ˈæktɪveɪt] v. make something more active 激活

stimulus(stimuli (pl)) [ˈstɪmjʊləs] n. something which may speed up decisions 刺激

arousal [əˈraʊzl] n. a state of heightened physiological activity 觉醒

stimulation [ˌstɪmjʊˈleɪʃn] n. the act of stimulating 刺激

organism [ˈɔːɡənɪzəm] n. a living thing that has the ability to act independently 有机物

survival [səˈvaɪvl] n. remaining alive 幸存

evolutionary [ˌiːvəˈluːʃənəri] adj. relating to evolution or development 进化的

Phrases

as/so long as... 只要……

date back 追溯

temporal lobe 颞叶

be responsible for... 对……负责
goose bumps 鸡皮疙瘩

Task 5 Fill in the blanks with the words given below and change the word forms if necessary

1. Many international affairs have become more and more complicated with the _____ (involve) of the big powers.

2. It is critical that the relief materials must _____ (distribution) to those who badly need them.

3. It is obvious that the _____ (region) economy in the city has been advanced to a new stage by tourism industry.

4. An increasing number of policies came into effect to _____ (stimulus) the use of natural resources in moderation.

5. For different species, the friendly environment plays an important role in their _____ (evolutionary).

6. As for maths leaning, the strong _____ (able) to reason is absolutely needed.

7. It was lucky that a majority of victims _____ (survival) the earthquake last week.

8. Each member should fulfill his social _____ (responsible).

9. _____ (emotion) as the lady was, she still faced up to all the difficulties and setbacks in her life.

10. Do you know the device _____ (functional)?

Task 6 Choose the correct answer according to the passage

1. What are the functions of "music center" in the brain? _____
  A. handling with music   B. appreciating music
  C. composing music   D. both A and B

2. In the sentence of the third paragraph "But **it** works closely with areas in the frontal lobe responsible for forming meaningful musical structure", what does **it** refer to? _____
  A. temporal lobe   B. frontal lobe
  C. auditory area   D. the study

3. It can be inferred that the same region can be activated by all the following stimuli except _____.
  A. food   B. clothes   C. sex   D. music

4. For the organism's existence, it is essential for them to meet the needs of _____.
  A. music   B. food   C. sex   D. both B and C

5. What is the main idea of the passage? _____
  A. Music spreads among the crowds in an unique way
  B. Music instruments were invented many years ago
  C. It is about the mechanics of how the brain responds to music
  D. Stimulation for music is very critical for organisms' survival

Task 7 Translate the following sentences into Chinese

1. As long as we were given more time, we would definitely work out the solution to the difficulty.

2. If the steady growth of population in the world goes on, we will come to a global aging in the near future.

_____

3. An increasing number of college students are trying to make themselves responsible for the society and their families.

_____

4. The fact that he is frequently absent from lectures suggests that he does not pay much attention to his study.

_____

5. The police are searching for the evidence associated with the crime which the murder once committed.

_____

Passage B

Music and Creativity

From Mozart to Metallica, a great number of people enjoy listening to various types of music while they write or draw. Many believe that music helps **boost** creativity, but an international study conducted by English and Swedish researchers is challenging that **notion**.

Psychologists from the Lancaster University and the University of Central Lancashire said that their findings **indicated** that music actually **stymies** creativity.

To come to their conclusions, researchers had participants completed verbal insight problems **designed to inspire** creativity while sitting in a quiet room, and then again while the background music played. They found that background music "significantly **impaired**" the participants' ability to complete tasks associated with verbal creativity.

The research team also tested background noises such as those commonly heard in a library, but found that such noises had no impact on subjects' creativity.

The tasks were simple word games. For example, participants were given three words, such as dress, dial, and flower. Then, they were asked to find a single word associated with all three words that could be combined to form common phrases or words. The single word, in this case, would be "sun" (sundress, sundial, sunflower).

Participants completed the tasks in either a quiet room, or while **exposed to** three different types of music: music with unfamiliar lyrics, instrumental music, or music with familiar lyrics.

"We found strong evidence of impaired performance when playing background music in comparison to quiet background conditions." says co-author Dr. Neil of Lancaster University.

Dr. Neil and his **colleagues** theorized that music interferes with the verbal working memory processes of the brain, hindering creativity. Also, **as far as** the library background noises having seemingly no effect, the study's authors believe that the library noises create a "steady state" environment that doesn't disrupt **concentration**.

It's worth mentioning that even familiar music with well-known lyrics impaired participants' creativity, regardless of whether or not it **elicited** a positive reaction, or whether participants typically studied or created while listening to music.

"To conclude, the findings here challenge the popular view that music **enhances** creativity, and instead **demonstrate** that music, regardless of the presence of **semantic** content (no lyrics, familiar lyrics or unfamiliar lyrics), consistently disrupts creative performance in insight problem solving." the study reads.

New Words

boost [buːst] v. increase or be beneficial to something 提高
notion ['nəʊʃ(ə)n] n. a general inclusive idea 概念,观念
psychologist [saɪ'kɒlədʒɪst] n. the professional specializing in psychology 心理学家
indicate ['ɪndɪkeɪt] v. to show or suggest 指出,表明
stymie ['staɪmɪ] v. to prevent the progress of something 妨碍
inspire [ɪn'spaɪə] v. to encourage or stimulate someone 鼓励
impair [ɪm'peə(r)] v. to make worse or less effective 削弱
colleague ['kɒliːg] n. the workmate 同事
concentration ['kɒnsən'treɪʃən] n. the action of focusing on something 集中,专注
elicit [ɪ'lɪsɪt] v. to call forth emotions or feelings 引出
enhance [ɪn'hɑːns] v. to raise the level of something 提升
demonstrate ['demənstreɪt] v. to establish the validity of something 证明,表明
semantic [sɪ'mæntɪk] adj. relating to meaning 语义的

Phrases

be designed to 旨在
be exposed to... 暴露在……面前
as far as... 就……而言

Task 8 Fill in the blanks with the words given below and change the word forms if necessary

1. We all know that Jack is the most _____ (creativity) boy in our school.
2. It seems to be _____ (challenge) for such a little girl to say something in front of a large crowd.
3. They all felt surprised at the _____ (find) in the research conducted by the professor.
4. It could be safely _____ (conclusion) that what he said turned out to be true.
5. All the staff should be given the right to _____ (participant) in decision making in the company.
6. Looking back on history, we see _____ (inspire) is an important source of arts.

7. How the students _____ (performance) in the exam made the teacher satisfied.

8. If children are _____ (exposure) to movies associated with drugs and violence, they tend to commit crimes.

9. The role of friendship is _____ (evidence) in developing the students' physical and psychological well-being.

10. The scientist discovered the _____ (theorize) in his daily life by chance that is still applied today.

Task 9　Choose the correct answer according to the passage

1. In the sentence "but an international study conducted by English and Swedish researchers is challenging that **notion**", what does the **notion** refer to? _____
   A. an international study　　　　　　　B. the idea that music aids to improve creativity
   C. different kinds of music　　　　　　　D. English and Swedish researchers' conclusion

2. Compared with the noise in the library, background music has a _____ influence on subjects' creativity.
   A. greater　　　B. less　　　C. nearly equivalent　　　D. undecidable

3. In the testing task introduced in the fifth paragraph, if you are given three words such as cake, light, and walk, which word might be proper for you to choose? _____
   A. sun　　　B. star　　　C. moon　　　D. satellite

4. In the sentence "Dr. Neil and his colleagues theorized that music **interferes** with the verbal working memory processes of the brain, hindering creativity", what does the word "**interfere**" mean? _____
   A. disturb　　　B. provide　　　C. interact　　　D. comfort

5. Which of the following statements is true?
   A. Noise in the lab has little impact on creativity because it can echo indoor
   B. Instrumental music and familiar lyrics equally influence one's creativity
   C. The findings from Dr. Neil are coincident with the popular view
   D. All music has a negative impact on creativity

Part 4　Practice and Learn

Main Sentence Constituent(句子主干成分)

1. 主语

主语指句子所要描述的人或事物,通常位于句首;通常由名词或名词性结构充当。不定式、少数动名词、主语从句作句子主语时,通常使用形式主语 it 来调整和平衡句子结构。

Smoking does harm to our health.(动名词作主语)

It is essential *that college students should cultivate their social skills*.(主语从句作主语)

2. 谓语

谓语用来表述或说明主语的动作或状态,通常放在主语的后面。谓语有人称、数、时态、语态的变化。谓语均由动词充当,句子的时态和语态均通过句子谓语部分的形式来体现。

At the sight of the picture, the little girl *couldn't help* shedding tears.

The candidate *will deliver* a speech next week.

3. 宾语

宾语位于及物动词或介词的后面,用来表示动作所涉及的对象。宾语一般由名词或名词性结构充当。在含有宾语+宾语补足语的结构中,如果宾语是由不定式或宾语从句充当,通常用 it 作为形式宾语,而把真正的宾语放在补语后面,以平衡句子结构。

We all know that *English is a widely-used international language*.(宾语从句作宾语)

I think it wise *to learn more when you are young*.(真正的宾语为不定式)

4. 表语

表语用来说明主语的身份、性质、特征和状态,常位于系动词之后,形成主系表的结构。常见的系动词有 be, go, become, appear, remain, seem, look, sound, feel, get, taste, smell 等。

The problem is *whether they will support us*.(表语从句作表语)

My dream is *to become a qualified nurse*.(不定式作表语)

Task 10　Indicate the sentence elements of the parts in bold

1. Tom **is flying** to Shanghai as soon as he receives the application **letter** from his uncle-in-law next week.
2. These **experiences** will lay a good **foundation** for their promising future.
3. **Who will be chosen as our leader** is still **a secret**.
4. Did you **know** that all those foreigners **came** from a remote country?
5. The famous singer made **it** known **that he would give the performance**.
6. Though he is **old** enough, he remains **fresh and energetic**.
7. Mother is telling the **kids** some interesting **stories**.
8. **I** plan **to kick off the habit of smoking**.
9. The regional **economy** will play an important **role**.
10. Nobody **knows** what our **life** will be like in the next decade.

Part 5　Write and Learn

A Note for Sick Leave（病假条）

英文病假条是日常生活和工作中经常使用到的一种应用文体,其格式多采用私人信函的简易格式,通常包括以下 5 个部分:date（日期,新近阅读的病假条不需要写年份,通常位于病假条右上角）;salutation（称谓,以 dear 开头,以表对上级的尊重）;body（正文,包含请假的病因、时间、提供的证明以及表达准假谢意和工作安排等基本信息）;complimentary（敬语）;signature（署名,通常位于病假条右下角）。

【Sample】

假定你是玛丽,昨天下午你在下班回家的路上骑自行车摔倒并骨折,欲向领导约翰申请 3 天的病假,请你代表玛丽给约翰写一则病假条。

写作要点:1.字数 80 左右。
　　　　　2.可以适当增加细节,以使行文连贯。
　　　　　3.注意病假条的格式。

参考词汇:bone fracture 骨折　　medical certificate 医疗证明

June 5th

Dear Mr. John,

    I am writing to ask for a sick leave of 3 days as I fell off the bike and got a bone fracture on my way back home from work yesterday afternoon. It starts from the 5th and ends with the 7th, both days inclusive. The medical certificate from the doctor has been enclosed.

    I would be obliged if you can grant me the leave. As for the missing work during my absence, I will try to make it up when I get back to work.

Yours sincerely,
Mary

Task 11　Try to write a note of sick leave based on the information given below

请代表王明于10月14日给李老师写一则英文病假条,基本内容如下:因感冒发烧明天无法到校上课;医生建议卧床休息2天;附带医学证明;希望准假,耽误的功课自己空闲时间弥补。

Unit 3 Health

Learning Objectives:

To *describe* parts of hand in English.

To *acquire* practical knowledge about personal hygiene by learning passage A.

To *improve* reading skills by scanning and to *grasp* the main idea of passage B.

To *grasp* the basic grammar rules about voices.

To *learn* to write English E-mails.

Part 1 Look and Learn

Warming-up: Look at the following pictures, talk about them and then finish Task 1

handwashing

liquid soap

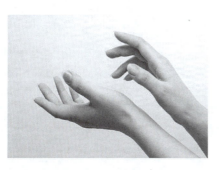

palm

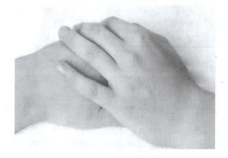

opisthenar

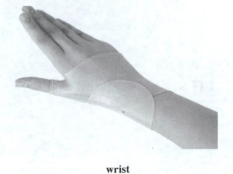
wrist

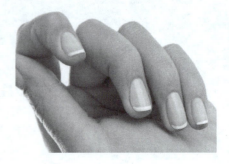
finger

New Words

soap [səʊp] n. a substance that you use with water for washing your body 肥皂

palm [pɑːm] n. the inner surface of the hand between the wrist and the fingers 手掌

wrist [rɪst] n. a joint between the hand and the arm 手腕

finger [ˈfɪŋɡə(r)] n. one of the four long thin parts that stick out from the hand (or five, if the thumb is included) 手指

Task 1 Match the words in the left column with the explanations in the right column

1. hand sanitizer	A. the practice of keeping yourself and your living and working areas clean in order to prevent illness and disease
2. fingertip	B. a supplement or alternative to soap and water for handwashing
3. hygiene	C. the thin hard areas at the end of each of your fingers
4. thumb	D. the end of the finger that is the furthest from the hand
5. fingernail	E. the short thick finger at the side of the hand, slightly apart from the other four fingers

Part 2 Speak and Learn

Task 2 Complete the conversation with the following expressions

A. Turn on

B. germs

C. the first thing

D. have a piece of bread

E. rub and rinse

Mom: Oscar, it's time to have lunch. Come back.

Oscar: OK, mom. Can I 1._____?

Mom: Oh, no.

Oscar: Why, mom?

Mom: There are a lot of 2._____ on your hands when you come home, Oscar.

Oscar: But I can't see germs.

Mom: Well, you can't see them because they are tiny. Still, they are bad for your health.

Oscar: Oh. I know, mom. My hands are too dirty. I should wash them first.

Mom: Yes. Do you know how to properly wash your hands?

Oscar: Oh, get hands wet and use enough soap to wash my hands.

Mom: That's not enough, my dear.

Oscar: Mom, can you tell me again? I really can't remember all of them.

Mom: OK, just do it follow me. Could you roll your sleeves up? 3. _____ the tap first and wet the hands. And then apply some liquid soap, and 4. _____ your hands. Finally, wash all the foam away and dry your hands. Oh, never forget to turn off the tap.

Oscar: Look, mom. Are they clean?

Mom: Mm, very clean. So, you'd better remember what 5. _____ is to do when you come back home.

Oscar: Wash my hands. Now, can I have some bread?

Mom: Of course.

Task 3 Answer the following questions according to the dialogue in no more than 3 words

1. Where does this conversation take place?

   This conversation takes place _____.

2. When does this conversation take place?

   It's probably about _____.

3. What does the mother ask Oscar to do before lunch?

   The mother asks him to _____ before lunch.

4. What does the mother tell her son not to forget after washing his hands?

   Dry his hands and never forget to _____ the tap.

5. How does the mother require her son to wash his hands?

   She wants her son to wash his hands _____.

Task 4 Talk with your partners about how to clean hands with the help of the following expressions

1. It's time to...

2. Do you know how to wash/clean...?

3. Would you like to...?

4. Wash all the foam away/off.

5. Roll up your sleeves first.

6. Turn on/off the tap.

Part 3   Read and Learn

Passage A

Mixed Opinions towards Dirt

In most people's view, **removing** dirt is a good thing. However, people's **attitude** towards dirt is not fixed.

Dirt on the skin was considered a way to block diseases, and the medical opinion was that **wash**ing **away** dirt with hot water would open up the skin and let the diseases in during the early 16th century. Public bathrooms were considered particularly dangerous. By 1538, the King of France had closed the

扫码听
课文A

bathrooms in his kingdom, before the King of England did in 1546. So, it began a long period when the rich and the poor lived with dirt in a friendly way in Europe. King Henry Ⅳ of France was famous for being dirty. After learning that a **nobleman** had taken a bath, the King **commanded** that nobleman should not go out to avoid the **attack** of diseases.

Although the belief in the advantages of dirt is long-standing, dirt has no longer been considered a good neighbor since the 18th century. **Scientifically** speaking, cleaning up dirt **is good for** health. Supplying clean water and washing hands are practical means to prevent diseases. Since the Second World War, however, it seems that cleaning standards have gone beyond science. The idea of advertising repeated sales is that the clothes should be whiter than white, softer cloth and **shiny** on the surface. Has the hate for dirt gone too far?

Today, people still have different attitudes towards dirt. First-time parents try to **keep** their children **away from** the soil, which may be the cause of the spread of diseases. Instead, an American **immunologist** encouraged children to play in the soil to build a strong **immune** system, while the latter position is gaining some ground.

New Words

remove [rɪˈmuːv] v. to take something or somebody away from a place 移开,去掉
attitude [ˈætɪtjuːd] n. the way that you think and feel about something or somebody 态度
nobleman [ˈnəʊblmən] n. a man who was a member of the nobility (男)贵族
command [kəˈmɑːnd] v. to tell somebody to do something 命令
attack [əˈtæk] v. to use violence to try to hurt or kill somebody 袭击,攻击
scientifically [ˌsaɪənˈtɪfɪkli] adv. involving science 科学地
shiny [ˈʃaɪni] adj. smooth and bright; reflecting the light 光亮的,锃亮的
immunologist [ˌɪmjʊˈnɒlədʒɪst] n. a medical scientist who specializes in immunology 免疫学专家
immune [ɪˈmjuːn] adj. cannot catch or be affected by a particular disease 免疫的

Phrases

wash away 冲走,清洗,消除
be good for 有益于,对……有好处
keep away from 远离,回避

Task 5　Fill in the blanks with the words given below and change the word forms if necessary

1. Four children _____ (remove) from the school for persistent bad behavior.
2. The military _____ (command) by general Washington.
3. Although he was _____ (noble) of birth, he lived as a poor man.

4. This blood test will show whether or not you _____ (immune) to the disease.
5. Rinsing with ice-cold water after a shampoo will give you _____ (shiny) hair.
6. Liver and kidney are _____ (particular) rich in vitamin A.
7. We are _____ (consider) buying a new car.
8. The treatment should _____ (repeat) every three to four hours.
9. My parents _____ always _____ (encourage) me in my choice of career.
10. Some people do _____ (gain) weight after they stop smoking.

Task 6 Choose the correct answer according to the passage

1. Why did the Kings of France and England in the 16th century close bathrooms? _____
   A. Because they thought that bathrooms were too dirty to stay in
   B. Because they believed that diseases could be spread in public bathrooms
   C. Because they considered bathing as the cause of skin disease
   D. Because they lived healthily in a dirty environment

2. What was Henry IV's attitude towards bathing? _____
   A. uninterested   B. curious   C. afraid   D. approving

3. What is the author's purpose in writing this article? _____
   A. To stress the role of dirt
   B. To call attention to the danger of dirt
   C. To introduce the history of dirt
   D. To present the changes of views on dirt

4. What was the immunologist's reason to encourage children to play in the soil? _____
   A. She thought that it would build a strong immune system
   B. She thought that the children like to play outdoors
   C. She thought that they do not have toys to play
   D. She thought that they should listen to adults

5. How does the passage mainly develop? _____
   A. by providing examples   B. by making comparisons
   C. by following the order of importance D. by following the order of time

Task 7 Translate the following sentences into Chinese

1. Even if you have had a regular physical check-up recently, you should still seek a medical opinion.

_____

2. The virus seems to have attacked his throat and stomach.

_____

3. He looks like a nobleman with his rich clothes.

_____

4. I am immune from the disease, for I had it once.

_____

5. A lot of drivers have serious attitude problems.

_____

Passage B

Keeping Clean

Having a daily hygiene **routine**, in addition to eating healthily and taking regular exercise, keeps a teen's body clean and free from smells. Additionally, good hygiene improves a teen's mental well-being and can boost confidence.

Personal hygiene

Poor personal hygiene can be unhealthy, and can increase the risk of **infection**, so it's a good idea for teens to **get into** healthy **habits** as soon as possible.

Hair

During **puberty**, the overproduction of sebum (oil) at the root of hair **follicles** can make hair greasy and lank, or bind dead skin cells together, causing dandruff.

To avoid these **afflictions**, wash hair regularly with a small amount of shampoo and rinse thoroughly. Some people need to wash their hair every day, while others can go a week or more before they need to wash their hair.

Eyes

Washing the hands before touching the eyes reduces the risk of **conjunctivitis**, also known as "pink eye" as well as other infections. Visiting the doctor regularly for a check-up is important, particularly if a teen wears contact lenses or glasses.

Skin and nails

Skin is the body's largest organ, so it's essential to keep it healthy. **Exfoliating** once a week and using a gentle scrub cream will remove dead skin cells, but avoid doing this more frequently as it could cause dryness and **irritation**. Moisturizing regularly keeps skin hydrated. Use a short-bristle brush to keep the nails and toenails clean.

Teeth

To keep the mouth healthy, it's best to brush the teeth and gums at least twice a day. Using floss to remove any trapped food between the teeth will help to prevent tooth **decay**. Sweets and sugary drinks should **be limited to** an occasional treat.

Armpit

The armpits are full of sweat-producing glands. The warm environment of the armpits is ideal for bacteria to break the sweat down, which can **lead to** unpleasant smells in this part of the body.

To minimize body **odour**, wash the armpits every day with warm water and mild soap. Most people use **deodorant** daily to help limit the amount they sweat, and to **cover up** any unpleasant smells.

Feet

There are more sweat glands on the **soles** of the feet than anywhere else on the human body, which is the reason that they are often the smelliest part.

Wash feet with warm and soapy water, and dry them thoroughly, especially between the toes, to prevent fungal infections, such as athlete's foot.

New Words

routine [ruːˈtiːn] n. the normal way in which you regularly do things 常规，惯例
infection [ɪnˈfekʃn] n. the act or process of causing or getting a disease 感染
infect [ɪnˈfekt] v. to make a disease spread to a person or a plant 感染
puberty [ˈpjuːbəti] n. when the body starts to become mature 青春期
follicle [ˈfɒlɪkl] n. the small holes in the skin, especially one that a hair grows from （毛）囊
affliction [əˈflɪkʃn] n. (formal) pain and suffering or something that causes it 折磨
conjunctivitis [kənˌdʒʌŋktɪˈvaɪtɪs] n. a disease that causes swelling in the eye 结膜炎
exfoliate [eksˈfəʊlieɪt] v. to remove dead cells from the surface of skin 使死皮脱落
irritation [ˌɪrɪˈteɪʃn] n. a feeling of slight pain and discomfort 刺激，疼痛
decay [dɪˈkeɪ] v. to be destroyed gradually by natural processes 腐烂，腐朽
odour [ˈəʊdə(r)] n. a smell, especially one that is unpleasant 臭味
deodorant [diˈəʊdərənt] n. a substance that people prevent unpleasant smells 除味剂
sole [səʊl] n. the bottom surface of the foot 脚掌，脚底（板）

Phrases

get into...habits 养成……的习惯
be limited to 限于
lead to 导致，通向
cover up 遮盖，掩饰

Task 8 Fill in the blanks with the words given below and change the word forms if necessary

1. It's very _____ (health) to be afraid when there is something to be afraid of.
2. Our teacher wants us to feel _____ (confidence) about asking questions when we don't understand.
3. Air, water, clothing and insects are all means of _____ (infect).
4. The meeting was very _____ (product). Both sides felt satisfied with all the agreements reached.
5. There are two main problems which _____ (affliction) people with hearing impairments.
6. Buses run _____ (frequent) between the city and the airport.
7. Some drugs can _____ (irritation) the lining of the stomach.
8. The traditional cinema seems to _____ (decay).
9. Wash your hands thoroughly with hot _____ (soap) water before handling any food.
10. She _____ (regular) appears on TV talk shows.

Task 9 Choose the correct answer according to the passage

1. Which one of the following can't help us develop the good hygiene habits in daily life? _____
   A. eating healthily   B. taking regular exercise
   C. having strong smell   D. keeping body clean

27

2. Why should teenagers develop healthy routine? _____

A. Personal hygiene contributes to growth for teens

B. Personal hygiene can reduce the risk of infection

C. Poor personal hygiene can be unhealthy

D. Parents ask teenagers to take care of personal hygiene

3. What is the purpose of washing hands before touching the eyes? _____

A. To form good habits through washing hands

B. To visit the optician regularly

C. To look cleaner and protect eyesight

D. To reduce the risk of conjunctivitis and other infections

4. Which part of the body is filled with sweat glands? _____

A. hair   B. skin   C. armpit   D. teeth

5. How can people prevent fungus infections? _____

A. Wash feet with warm and soapy water   B. Don't dress too much

C. Take shower more often   D. Do exercise regularly

Part 4　Practice and Learn

Voice(语态)

英语的语态有两种：主动语态和被动语态。主动语态表示主语是动作的执行者，被动语态表示主语是动作的承受者。

The successful businessman **motivated** the younger generation.

The younger generation **was motivated** by the successful businessman.

被动语态的基本结构：**be＋p. p**(**past participle**，过去分词)。一般来说，大多数时态有其主动和被动结构(表 3-1)。

表 3-1　时态/语态一览表

时　态	主 动 结 构	被 动 结 构
一般现在时	v(动词原形)	am/is/are＋p. p
一般过去时	v-ed(过去式)	was/were＋p. p
一般将来时	will/shall＋v	will/shall＋be＋p. p
现在进行时	am/is/are＋v-ing	am/is/are＋being＋p. p
过去进行时	was/were＋v-ing	was/were＋being＋p. p
将来进行时	will/shall＋be＋v-ing	will/shall＋be＋p. p (用一般将来时的被动语态代替)
现在完成时	have/has＋p. p	have/has＋been＋p. p
过去完成时	had＋p. p	had＋been＋p. p
将来完成时	will/shall＋have＋p. p	will/shall＋have＋been＋p. p
过去将来时	would＋v	would＋be＋p. p
现在完成进行时	have/has＋been＋v-ing	have/has＋been＋p. p (用现在完成时的被动语态代替)
情态动词	can/may/must＋v	can/may/must＋be＋p. p

将主动句变为被动句时应观察主动句的时态,将主动句的宾语提前充当被动句的主语,谓语部分使用与之相对应的被动结构。被动句的时态通常要求与主动句的时态保持一致。

He is painting the doors with a brush.

The doors are being painted with a brush.

The teacher has translated the novel into French.

The novel has been translated into French (by the teacher).

Task 10　Fill in the blanks with the corrective voice

1. Chopsticks ＿＿＿＿＿＿＿＿＿＿(use) by Chinese people.
2. Our classroom ＿＿＿＿＿＿＿＿＿＿(clean) every day.
3. Tom's bicycle ＿＿＿＿＿＿＿＿＿＿(steal) just now.
4. A sports meeting ＿＿＿＿＿＿＿＿＿＿(hold) in our school the day after tomorrow.
5. A lecture is ＿＿＿＿＿＿＿＿＿＿(give) by a famous professor tomorrow afternoon.
6. My book ＿＿＿＿＿＿＿＿＿＿(lose), so I can't finish my homework.
7. The lunch ＿＿＿＿＿＿＿＿＿＿(prepare) well when he arrived home.
8. Nobody ＿＿＿＿＿＿＿＿＿＿(look) down upon.
9. My car needs ＿＿＿＿＿＿＿＿＿＿(repair).
10. The storybook ＿＿＿＿＿＿＿＿＿＿(sell) well.

Part 5　Write and Learn

E-mail(电子邮件)

随着时代的发展,人们在日常生活工作中经常使用 E-mail。它的基本格式包括收件人(to...)、发件人(from...)、主题(subject),正文内容与书信基本一致。

【Sample】

假定你是小岚,根据以下内容以第一人称发一封英文 E-mail。发件人:小岚。收件人:Susan。发件人的 E-mail 地址:Vivian@163.com。收件人的 E-mail 地址:Susan008@hotmail.com。

小岚在某网站(www.amazon.cn)上卖出了一本书,该书为《中医基础理论》。买家是来自美国的 Susan。小岚感谢 Susan 购买此书,并将书寄出,预计五天内到达。她希望 Susan 收到书后在网站上留下反馈意见。如果满意,希望 Susan 向其他客户推荐。小岚最近还会出售一些新的书,若再次购买可以享受折扣。

Words for reference:

反馈意见 feedback;《中医基础理论》Basic Theory of Traditional Chinese Medicine

From:Vivian@163.com

To:Susan008@hotmail.com

Subject:For thanks

Dear Ms. Susan,

　　How do you do! First of all, thank you for buying the book *Basic Theory of Traditional Chinese Medicine* on Amazon. The book has been sent to you and it could arrive in five days. Hopefully, would you give us online feedback after you receive the book? What's more, if you feel great with the book, we also hope you would recommend it to your friends. Finally, you're welcome to buy some new books which will be available recently. Surely you will enjoy some discounts if you buy them.

Sincerely yours,
Xiao Lan

Task 11 Try to write an E-mail based on the information given below

假设你是王星,你想发一封 E-mail 给教授史密斯先生,向他咨询一些学业上的问题,并请他推荐几本如何写好论文的书籍。

发件人:王星。收件人:Smith。发件人的 E-mail 地址:Wangxingfire@163.com。

收件人的 E-mail 地址:Smith321@163.com。

Unit 4   Food

Learning Objectives:

To **describe** different kinds of food and eating habits in English.
To **know** about food allergies in daily life according to the information in passage A.
To **improve** reading speed by scanning and to **understand** the main idea of passage B.
To **grasp** the basic grammar rules related to sentence tense in English.
To **learn** to write an English congratulation letter.

Part 1   Look and Learn

Warming-up: Look at the following pictures, talk about them and then finish Task 1

beef

noodle

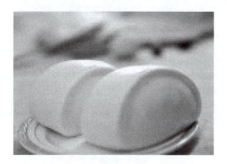

steamed bread

bean curd

chicken

stuffed buns

New Words

noodle ['nu:d(ə)l] n. a ribbonlike strip of pasta 面条

chicken ['tʃɪkɪn] n. the flesh of a chicken used for food 鸡，鸡肉

curd [kɜːd] n. coagulated milk, used to make cheese 凝乳

steam [stiːm] v. cook food with the hot gas produced when water boils 蒸

stuffed [stʌft] adj. filled with something 已经喂饱了的，塞满了的

Task 1 Match the words in the left column with the explanations in the right column

1. cauliflower	A. a plant whose succulent young shoots are cooked and eaten as a vegetable
2. beef	B. the portion of the loin (especially of beef) just in front of the rump
3. asparagus	C. cattle that are reared for their meat
4. sirloin	D. carotenoid that makes tomatoes red; may lower the risk of prostate cancer
5. lycopene	E. a plant having a large edible head of crowded white flower buds

Part 2 Speak and Learn

Task 2 Complete the conversation with the following expressions

A. we can share

B. a little shorter

C. delicious and appetizing

D. a second helping

E. For staple food

Li Lei: All the food smells tasty today and makes my mouth water.

Wang Jun: Let's line up here. This line seems 1. _____.

Li Lei: What's on the menu today?

Wang Jun: Fish, beef, chicken, bean curd, cauliflower and fruits. 2. _____ we have rice, steamed bread, stuffed buns and noodles.

Li Lei: Oh, we're lucky today, aren't we?

Wang Jun: I'd rather take stewed cabbage with beef.

Li Lei: I think I'll take fried fish, because fish is one of my favorites.

Wang Jun: That's good, 3. _____ what we have. Here we are. You go ahead.

(They get everything ready.)

Li Lei: Here is a free table. Let's sit down. Help yourself to some fish, please. Isn't it 4._____?

Wang Jun: I'm sorry. I don't like. It's a little too salty.

Li Lei: I see. You people from south prefer sweet, don't you?

Wang Jun: Yes, I like the fish cooked in sweet and sour sauce best. Try some beef, please.

Li Lei: Thank you. I'm through with one steamed bread and I'd like 5._____.

Wang Jun: Your appetite is good.

Li Lei: I'm always feeling hungry.

Task 3 Answer the following questions according to the dialogue in no more than 3 words

1. Where does this conversation take place?

   This conversation takes place _____.

2. Besides staple food, what dishes are available that day?

   Fish, beef, chicken, bean curd, _____.

3. What did Li Lei order?

   He ordered _____ with beef.

4. What did Wang Jun order?

   He ordered _____.

5. Did Wang Jun like fish? Why?

   Yes, because fish is one of _____.

Task 4 Discuss with your partners about the different eating habits between people from North China and those from South China with the help of the following expressions

1. What food do you like...?

2. How do you think...?

3. What/How about salt/sweet/spicy food...?

4. The food culture of northerners/southerners is...

5. Do you have any tips on...?

Part 3 Read and Learn

Passage A

Are We Becoming More Allergic to Food?

As we all know, eating too much the wrong kind of food can **be bad for** our health, but for some people having a food **allergy** means eating certain things can actually **be harmful**—and now, it seems that this is affecting more and more of us.

An allergy is caused by the **immune system** fighting substances in the environment, known as allergens, which should be seen as **harmless**. Food allergies can cause life-threatening reactions, which means people have to spend their lives following strict dietary **restrictions**. We often hear about people having allergies to dairy products and to peanuts. Last year a 15-year-old girl died after suffering a fatal **allergic** reaction from eating a baguette containing **sesame seeds**. This led to calls for better **food**

labeling laws.

Research has found that this problem is **particularly** affecting children. Writing for the BBC website, Dr. Alexandra Santos from King's College London says, "food allergy now affects about 7 percent of children in the UK and 9 percent of children in Australia, for example. Across Europe, 2 percent of adults have food allergies".

So what might be the cause? Dr. Santos says that the increase in allergies is not simply the effect of society becoming more **aware of** them and better at diagnosing them, it seems to be more environmental. She says, "possible factors are pollution, dietary changes and less **exposure** to **microbes**, which change the respond of our immune systems". She points out that it's very common for migrants who move to another country to develop **asthma** and food allergies in their new location.

A lot of work is being done to try and find a cure, but that's not easy. So for now allergy sufferers must watch what they eat and rely on clear and accurate labeling.

New Words

allergy [ˈælədʒɪ] n. hypersensitivity reaction to a particular allergen 过敏

harmless [ˈhɑːmlɪs] adj. not causing or capable of causing harm 无害的, 不致伤的

restriction [rɪˈstrɪkʃən] n. a principle that limits the extent of something 限制, 约束

allergic [əˈlɜːdʒɪk] adj. characterized or caused by allergy 过敏的

sesame [ˈsesəmɪ] n. a herb grown for its small oval seeds and its oil 芝麻

seed [siːd] n. a small round or oval object produced by a plant and from which, when it is planted, a new plant can grow 种子, 籽

particularly [pəˈtɪkjʊləlɪ] adv. to a distinctly greater extent or degree than common 特别地, 独特地

exposure [ɪkˈspəʊʒə] n. when someone experiences something or is affected by it because he or she is in a particular situation or place 暴露, 曝光

microbe [ˈmaɪkrəʊb] n. a minute life form (especially a disease-causing bacterium) 微生物, 细菌

asthma [ˈæsmə] n. respiratory disorder characterized by wheezing 气喘, 哮喘

Phrases

be bad for 对……不利
be harmful 对……有害
immune system 免疫系统
food labeling 食品标签
be aware of 意识到

Task 5 Fill in the blanks with the words given below and change the word forms if necessary

1. We need more _____ (restriction) on industrial polluters.
2. Many people are _____ (allergy) to airborne pollutants such as pollen.
3. The film's special effects are _____ (particular) impressive.
4. He claims television violence is _____ (harm) to children.
5. There was a close relationship between soil _____ (microbe) biomass and soil enzyme.
6. He is _____ (suffer) from the loss of his old friend.
7. Allergy to cats is one of the commonest causes of _____ (asthma).
8. The incident showed that their leaders were not _____ (immune) to corruption.
9. Significant _____ (exposure) to toxic compounds present unacceptable risks.
10. The _____ (seed) were not meant for human consumption.

Task 6 Choose the correct answer according to the passage

1. How do you understand "food allergy"? _____
   A. Smelling certain things can actually be harmful
   B. Eating certain things can actually be harmful
   C. Touching certain things can actually be harmful
   D. Eating certain things cannot actually be harmful
2. What food would people be possibly allergic to? _____
   A. dairy products   B. peanuts   C. sesame seeds   D. all above
3. For the migrants who move to another country, apart from food allergies, what is the most likely to happen? _____
   A. asthma   B. diarrhea   C. vomitus   D. nervous breakdown
4. What are the possible factors of food allergy? _____
   A. pollution   B. dietary changes
   C. less exposure to microbes   D. all above
5. What is the percentage of adults across Europe having food allergies? _____
   A. 3%   B. 7%   C. 2%   D. 9%

Task 7 Translate the following sentences into Chinese

1. Not all chemicals normally present in living organisms are harmless.
   _____
2. Although deeply shamed by his exposure, he bounced back.
   _____
3. To speed up germination, it is worth soaking the seed in water.
   _____
4. Allergy to cats is one of the commonest causes of asthma.
   _____
5. The incidents showed that their leaders were not immune to corruption.
   _____

Passage B

Food and Health

With today's way of life, people are more likely to suffer from **obesity**, be exposed to various diseases or contract some forms of cancer. **On the other hand**, modern medicine has **evolved** so that people can **rely on** the latest drugs or **devices** to treat cancer.

When it comes to treating cancer, prevention and **detection** is probably the best way to nip it in its bud. Thus, we should always go for regular health screenings to detect cancer in its early stage and **isolate** it early. Here are four kinds of food that are good for our health.

1. Carrots

Even though carrots are mainly thought to be good for one's eye sight, research from the last ten years suggests that they are also good against some types of cancer, including **prostate** cancer.

A study was done in mice which were fed an increased carrot intake, and the study showed that carrots could stop the growth of prostate cancer. Carrot have many other health benefits too, so there is no reason not to eat them!

2. Broccoli

Broccoli is one of the best natural cancer fighters against many types of cancer. **Colon** cancer and bladder cancer are among the top two cancers that can be treated or even prevented when eating broccoli. Find it in whichever form you can, and be it fresh, frozen or pre-cooked, it will still retain most of its nutritional value! The high fibre level in broccoli can also help with your digestion, so broccoli is a vegetable that **is beneficial for** your health to eat often.

3. Tomatoes

Tomatoes are healthy and tasty at the same time. Cooked tomatoes help your body release more **lycopene**, a specific phytochemical that provides cancer fighting benefits.

Tomatoes also provide you with lots of **antioxidants** for your body, and are known to be useful to treat or prevent prostate cancer. There are many ways to eat tomatoes. It can be eaten raw or cooked with dishes, or blended to make juice as well.

4. Walnuts

Do you want to prevent breast cancer or prostate cancer? Walnuts may be your answer. They also contain lots of omega 3 (a type of fatty acids) that is actually beneficial to our health such as lowering our risk of **coronary** heart disease and reducing high level of **cholesterol**. Walnuts are great as a breakfast food or as a **snack** in between meals.

New Words

obesity [ə(ʊ)ˈbiːsətɪ] n. more than average fatness 肥胖,肥胖症
evolve [ɪˈvɒlv] v. work out 发展,进化,使逐步形成
device [dɪˈvaɪs] n. an instrument invented for a particular purpose 装置
detection [dɪˈtekʃ(ə)n] n. the perception that something has occurred 侦查,察觉
isolate [ˈaɪsəleɪt] v. place or set apart 使隔离,使孤立
prostate [ˈprɒsteɪt] n. a firm partly muscular chestnut sized gland in males at the neck of the urethra 前列腺
broccoli [ˈbrɒkəlɪ] n. a plant with dense clusters of tight green flower buds 西蓝花
colon [ˈkəʊlən] n. the part of the intestine between the cecum and the rectum 结肠
lycopene [ˈlaɪkəpiːn] n. carotenoid that makes tomatoes red 番茄红素
antioxidant [ˌæntɪˈɒksɪd(ə)nt] n. substance that inhibits oxidation 抗氧化剂
coronary [ˈkɒrən(ə)rɪ] adj. the blood vessels surrounding the heart clot (thrombus) 冠状动脉或静脉的
cholesterol [kəˈlestərɒl] n. an animal sterol normally synthesized by the liver 胆固醇
snack [snæk] n. a light informal meal 小吃,快餐

Phrases

on the other hand 另一方面
rely on 依靠,依赖
be beneficial for 对……有益

Task 8 Fill in the blanks with the words given below and change the word forms if necessary

1. The excessive consumption of sugar leads to problems of _____ (obese).
2. Herbs for the _____ (prevent) of encephalitis can be found everywhere in this area.
3. Water is a compound _____ (contain) the elements hydrogen and oxygen.

4. That is highly _____ (risk) if they take their entire client base away from one medium.

5. The study found that the patients' brisk of _____ (suffer) a fall was higher for up to one hour after emotional stress.

6. The bright plumage of many male birds has _____ (evolve) to attract the females.

7. David had to be _____ (isolate) for whooping cough.

8. The most important deterrent for criminals is the likelihood of _____ (detection) and arrest.

9. Mr. Harper has been the main cause and _____ (benefit) of that process.

10. _____ (antioxidant) compounds in tea can help to inhibit the growth of tumors.

Task 9 Choose the correct answer according to the passage

1. What disease is the highest risk among obese people? _____
   A. cancer   B. headache   C. fever   D. dead
2. Which of the following is eating more carrots good to? _____
   A. foot   B. ear   C. nose   D. eye
3. What content of broccoli is very high and can promote peristalsis? _____
   A. fat   B. fibre   C. protein   D. carbohydrate
4. What can be used to prevent and treat prostate cancer in tomatoes? _____
   A. starch   B. ester   C. protein   D. antioxidants
5. Which of the following can help prevent breast cancer and prostate cancer? _____
   A. carrots   B. broccoli   C. walnuts   D. tomatoes

Part 4   Practice and Learn

Sentence Tense(句子时态)

句子的时态是句子的谓语动词所表示的动作发生的时间状态。任何一个英语句子都有它的时态和语态。时态和语态都是通过句子的谓语部分的形式来反映(即句子的谓语部分的形式不同,说明句子的时态或语态有差异)。时间状态(过去、现在、将来)与动作状态(一般、进行、完成)相组合,可以形成英语中的多种时态形式。时间状语(含时间状语从句)是考虑时态选用的重要依据。

观察下列三组句子谓语部分的形式并思考句子间时态和语态的差异。

第一组 They **are discussing** the topic in the lecture hall now.

The topic **is being discussed** in the lecture hall now.

第二组 They **will discuss** the topic in the lecture hall next week.

They **were discussing** the topic in the lecture hall this time yesterday.

第三组 The topic **will be discussed** in the lecture hall next week.

The topic **was being discussed** in the lecture hall this time yesterday.

第一组 2 个句子时态一样(均为现在进行时),语态不一样;第二组 2 个句子时态不一样,语态一样(均为主动语态);第三组 2 个句子时态不一样,语态一样(均为被动语态)。

英语中最常见的时态形式

英语中最常见 16 种时态形式,即 4 个一般时态(一般现在时、一般过去时、一般将来时、一般过去将来时)、4 个进行时态(现在进行时、过去进行时、将来进行时、过去将来进行时,均含现在分词)、4 个完成时态(现在完成时、过去完成时、将来完成时、过去将来完成时,均含过去分词)、4个组合时态(现在完成进行时、过去完成进行时、将来完成进行时、过去将来完成进行时)(表4-1)。

表4-1 英语中的16种时态形式(以 study 为例)

时态(tense)	一般时	进行时	完成时	完成进行时
现在	study studies	am studying is studying are studying	have studied has studied	have been studying has been studying
过去	studied	was studying were studying	had studied	had been studying
将来	shall study will study	shall be studying will be studying	shall have studied will have studied	shall have been studying will have been studying
过去将来	should study would study	should be studying would be studying	should have studied would have studied	should have been studying would have been studying

1. 过去完成时

结构:**had**(助动词)+**p. p**(过去分词)

By the end of last month, they had finished writing their graduation thesis.

用法:任何时候使用该时态,一定能体现"过去之过去"这一概念,即在某一过去的时间或动作之前所发生的行为。

The speaker told the public at the press conference that the nation had accomplished its expected targets.

(accomplish 先于过去的动作 tell 发生)

She complained that the vehicles **had made** much noise in the community.

(make 先于过去的动作 complain 发生)

2. 一般过去将来时

结构:**would**(助动词)+**v**(动词原形)(无人称和数的变换)

用法:在英语中单独使用过去将来时的情况比较少见,该时态多出现于含有宾语从句的复合句中,尤其是将直接引语变为间接引语的句子中。

She said, "I will work as a doctor in 2 years."

She said she **would work** as a doctor after 2 years.

He asked me, "Where shall I get the ticket for the play tomorrow?"

He asked me where he **would get** the ticket for the play the next day.

3. 现在完成进行时

结构:**have/has**(助动词)+**been**+**v-ing**(现在分词)

用法:该时态为组合时态,即由现在完成时和现在进行时2种时态组合而成,表示动作从过去开始持续到现在,到现在为止,该动作还在进行中。多用该时态来强调动作的持续发生,与一段时间状语连用。

We **have been utilizing** windmill to generate electricity for many years.

(强调 utilize 这个动作的持续发生,到现在为止,这个动作还在进行)

Tourism **has been advancing** some other industries all the way.

(强调 advance 这个动作的持续发生,到说这句话为止,这个动作还在进行)

Task 10　Choose the correct answer

1. Li Ming said he _____ happy if Brian _____ to China next month.

　　A. as, come　　　　　　　　　　B. was, would come

C. would be, came　　　　　　　　　　D. will be, come

2. Jenny said she _____ her holiday in China.

　A. spent　　　　　　　　　　　　　B. would spent
　C. was going to spent　　　　　　　D. would spend

3. —What did your son say in the letter?
　—He told me that he _____ the Disney World the next day.

　A. will visit　　B. would visit　　C. is going to visit　　D. has visited

4. He asked me _____ during the summer holidays.

　A. where I had been　　　　　　　B. where I had gone
　C. where had I been　　　　　　　D. where had I gone

5. What _____ Jane _____ by the time he went there?

　A. did, do　　B. has, done　　C. did, did　　D. had, done

6. I _____ 900 English words by the time I was ten.

　A. learned　　B. was learning　　C. had learned　　D. learn

7. She _____ lived here for _____ years.

　A. had, a few　　B. has, several　　C. had, a lot of　　D. has, a great deal of

8. —I'm sure Andrew will win the first prize in the final.
　—I think so. He _____ for it for months.

　A. is preparing　　　　　　　　　　B. was preparing
　C. had been preparing　　　　　　　D. has been preparing

9. By the time he realizes he _____ into a trap, it'll be too late for him to do anything about it.

　A. walks　　B. walked　　C. has walked　　D. had walked

10. —I have got a headache.
　—No, wonder. You _____ in front of that computer too long.

　A. work　　　　　　　　　　　　　B. are working
　C. have been working　　　　　　　D. worked

Part 5　Write and Learn

A Letter of Congratulation(祝贺信)

祝贺信是指在日常生活中,得知某人竞赛获奖、考上大学、结婚,以及在过新年或重大节日等时,给对方祝贺的信件。书写时应做到真诚、自然、亲切动人。

祝贺信通常包括以下内容:祝贺事由;被祝贺人所取得的成绩;被祝贺人过去的努力;被祝贺人的优点;表达自己的愿望。

开头常用句式

1. I feel very happy for your dream has come true.
2. I am writing to express my congratulation on your winning the place in the English speech contest.
3. Congratulations on your success in the National Entrance Examination.

常用语块

1. Congratulations on ...

2. ...come true
3. How happy I am to hear...
4. I have learned with delight that you...
5. I'm very happy for you(r)...
6. I would like to express my congratulations on...

结尾常用句式

1. Good luck!
2. I wish you success and fulfillment in the years ahead.
3. I feel very happy for your dream has come true.

【Sample】

假定你是李宾,你得知你的外国笔友Peter获得了世界大学生中文演讲比赛一等奖。你为他感到骄傲,并给他写一封祝贺信,要点如下:天天练习讲汉语,从不会到流利,终于成功;继续努力,有机会来中国留学;希望见面和交流。

注意:1. 词数100左右。

2. 可以适当增加细节,以使行文连贯。

3. 开头语和结束语已为你写好。

参考词汇:中文演讲比赛 Chinese speech contest

Dear Peter,

I would like to express my congratulations to you on your receiving the first prize of the Chinese speech contest. I know that you were not good at Chinese at first. However, you practiced speaking Chinese every day. As the saying goes, "Everything comes to him who waits." Finally, you succeeded! In my mind, this match is very difficult for a foreign student.

So I'm so surprised that you become champion of this competition. If you go on studying Chinese harder, you will have the opportunity to study in China. At last, I hope to see you and communicate with each other.

Sincere congratulations to you again!

Sincerely yours,

Li Bin

Task 11   Try to write a letter of congratulation based on the information given below

假定你是李宾,你得知你的好友刘强今年考上了北京大学(Peking University)。他来自贫困地区,是村里的第一位大学生。请你给他写一封祝贺信,要点如下:考上理想大学,父母骄傲;努力学习将来为家乡服务;对未来的祝福。

注意:1. 词数100左右。

2. 可以适当增加细节,以使行文连贯。

Unit 5 Family

Learning Objectives:

To *talk about* your apartment and your family in English.
To *cherish and value* the quality time with your family.
To *build* a constructive and harmonious relationship with your family members.
To *grasp* the basic grammar rules related to participles in English.
To *learn to write* an English letter asking for help.

Part 1   Look and Learn

Warming-up: Look at the following pictures, talk about them and then finish Task 1

living room

balcony

bedroom

dining room

kitchen

restroom

New Words

balcony ['bælkəni] n. a platform that is built on the upstairs outside wall of a building, with a wall or railing around it 阳台

bedroom ['bedrʊm] n. a room for sleeping in 卧室

kitchen ['kɪtʃin] n. a room in which meals are cooked or prepared 厨房

restroom ['restruːm] n. a room with a toilet in a public place, such as a theatre or a restaurant 洗手间，盥洗室

Task 1 Match the words in the left column with the explanations in the right column

1. granduncle	A. son of one's brother or sister
2. nephew	B. mother of one's husband or wife
3. mother-in-law	C. sister who has the same father or mother
4. half sister	D. child of one's uncle or aunt
5. cousin	E. uncle of one's father or mother

Part 2   Speak and Learn

Task 2 Complete the conversation with the following expressions

A. lies in

B. generation gap

C. in a house

D. burst into laughter

E. keep in touch

F. nice and tolerant

Steve: Hi, Emily. Where is your hometown?

Emily: I come from Chongqing, which 1. _____ southwest China.

Steve: Do you have any siblings?

Emily: Yes, I have a twin sister. This is my family photo.

Steve: Great! You and your sister look so identical. What type is your father? Are your father and mother hard on you?

Emily: Actually they are 2. _____ to me. We are like close friends. I believe there is no

扫码听对话

43

3. _____ in my family.

Steve: So lucky for you! Do you live in an apartment or a house?

Emily: We used to live 4. _____ ten years ago. When I started my primary school life, my family moved to a town and lived in an apartment. Anyway, we still miss the days in the countryside.

Steve: Me too! I prefer to enjoy the fresh air, green woods and quiet life there.

Emily: So how about you? What kind of person is your father?

Steve: He is an insightful man, always with new and creative ideas. I also like his humor, very relaxing and refreshing indeed, sometimes making us 5. _____.

Emily: Sounds good. How do you 6. _____ with them?

Steve: I call my parents twice a week. When time is available, I occasionally send hand-writing letters to them.

Emily: Cool! By the way, where are you from, Steve?

Steve: I come from Yunnan Province. Welcome to visit my hometown someday.

Emily: Thanks. I am expecting that.

Task 3 Answer the following questions according to the dialogue in no more than 3 words

1. Are Steve and Emily from the same part of China?

    Yes, they are. They both come from _____.

2. Does Emily look different from her sister?

    No. They look very _____.

3. What does Steve mean by saying his father is insightful.

    He means that his father has _____ ideas.

4. What make the two speakers like the life in the countryside?

    The fresh air, green woods and _____ there.

5. How often does Steve call his parents?

    He calls them _____.

Task 4 Talk with your partners about the appearance of one family member with the help of the following expressions

Here are several kinds of words and expressions for describing a person.

1. **General appearance**: pretty, handsome, good-looking, elegant, neatly-dressed.
2. **Build (shape)**: tall, short, medium height, overweight, plump, slim, skinny.
3. **Hair or beard**: long/short, curly/straight/wavy hair, bald, gray/white beard.
4. **Age**: little, teenager, young, middle-aged, old, in his or her (early/late) thirties.
5. **Personality**: humorous, perceptive, diligent, friendly, serious-looking, optimistic.

Part 3   Read and Learn

Passage A

Are We Spending More Time Alone?

Because of the spread of **coronavirus**, in many places around the world, we are being **urged** or even **mandated** to **practice social distancing**. For those of us who live alone, that could mean much more time

扫码听
课文A

Note

by ourselves.

In fact, long before the spread of coronavirus, the time we spend alone had been increasing **remarkably**. That's not just true for people who live alone. Single parents, couples without kids, and nuclear families with their parents and children all **under the same roof**—people in all of these kinds of **arrangements** have been spending more time alone.

Some related data were **impressive**. Here are some of the findings from a study about Finnish people. The amount of time that people spend alone has increased **dramatically**. Alone time increased the most for single people without kids. **Overall**, the amount of time that people spend alone increases with age. **On the average**, people who are **employed** spend less time alone than people who are unemployed.

In this study, only **physical togetherness** counted as time spent with other people. An unanswered question is how much of the time that people are spending on computers involves connecting with other people.

We cannot know that the amount of time that **Finnish** people spend alone **compares to** the amount of time that people spend alone in other countries from this study. There are other research comparing the time that children spend alone. As the note of this study, children in Finland spend an **average** of more than one **additional** hour alone every day compared to children in Spain or the UK.

New Words

coronavirus [kəˌrəʊnəˈvaɪərəs] n. a type of airborne virus 冠状病毒

urge [ɜːdʒ] v. to advise or try hard to persuade someone to do something 敦促,催促

mandate [ˈmændeɪt] v. to order somebody to behave or do something in a particular way 强制执行,委托办理

remarkably [rɪˈmɑːkəblɪ] adv. to a remarkable degree or extent 非常,显著地,格外

arrangement [əˈreɪndʒmənt] n. a plan or preparation which you make so that something will happen or be possible 安排,准备

impressive [ɪmˈpresɪv] adj. making a strong or vivid impression 给人印象深刻的

dramatically [drəˈmætɪklɪ] adv. a dramatic change or event happens suddenly and is very noticeable and surprising 突如其来地,急剧地

overall [ˈəʊvərɔːl] adv. generally; when you consider everything 一般来说,大体上

employ [ɪmˈplɔɪ] v. to give somebody a job to do for payment 雇用

togetherness [tə'geðərnɪs] n. the happy feeling you have when you are with people you like, especially family and friends(尤指家庭或朋友)和睦相处,亲密无间

Finnish ['fɪnɪʃ] n. belonging or relating to Finland or to its people, language, or culture 芬兰的,芬兰人的

average ['ævərɪdʒ] n. a level which is usual 平均水平,一般水准

additional [ə'dɪʃənl] adj. more than first mentioned or usual 附加的,额外的

Phrases

practice social distancing 保持社交距离
under the same roof 在同一屋檐下,同处一室
on the average 平均而言
physical togetherness 现实生活中的团聚
compare to 与……相比

Task 5 Fill in the blanks with the words given below and change the word forms if necessary

1. Practicing social _____(distance) after the outbreak of the epidemic is crucial.
2. They have made _____(remark) achievements in containing the virus.
3. The teacher had some students _____(arrangement) the classroom desks in a special way.
4. His remarks about the film are interesting and _____(impress).
5. _____(Finnish) is a northern European country where Santa Clause is said to live.
6. The number of confirmed cases in that area has increased _____(dramatic).
7. Due to rapid economic development in recent years, people in that city see the lowest _____(employ) rate.
8. Food _____(additional) are forbidden in the processing of food products to guarantee food safety in some countries.
9. The evidence collected so far shows that there is no _____(connect) between this kind of lifestyle and the increase of body weight.
10. _____(compare) speaking, men are more physically stronger than women.

Task 6 Choose the correct answer according to the passage

1. According to the passage, which of the following statements is true? _____
A. Before the coronavirus, people spent more time together
B. Before the coronavirus, the time we spend alone had been going up greatly
C. After the coronavirus, we spend more time with other people
D. After the coronavirus, we practice social distancing so that we spend the same time alone

2. What does the writer mean by practicing social distancing? _____
A. Keeping some distance with your family members
B. Avoiding going to public gatherings or visiting crowded places
C. Volunteering to be social workers in the distant places
D. Isolating yourself in a health care institutions

3. What does the finding from the study about Finnish people show? _____
A. The amount of time that people spend alone has increased gradually
B. Alone time increased the most for unmarried people with kids
C. Generally speaking, the amount of time that people spend alone increases with age

D. On the average, working people spend more time alone than people who don't have jobs

4. According to the fourth paragraph, what question is still to be answered? _____
A. Should we spend so much time surfing the internet to make friends
B. How can we use computer to connect other people
C. How much time should we get involved in online chat with other people
D. How much time used on computers should be regarded as interpersonal connection

5. According to the study, in which country children spend most time alone? _____
A. Finland   B. China   C. Spain   D. the UK

Task 7 Translate the following sentences into Chinese

1. After the outbreak of coronavirus, the cities practiced lockdown and asked the residents to do social distancing.

_____

2. The population in that country has been decreasing remarkably in recent decades.

_____

3. The audience gave a like to her impressive speech because she used story-telling style and vivid description.

_____

4. The amount of money that the boy spent increased dramatically. It seemed that he just wanted to empty his parents bank account.

_____

5. On the average, people who are married spend less time travelling than people who are single.

_____

Passage B

Stories on a Headboard

The bed was about forty-five years old when Mom passed it along to me a few months after my father died. I decided to **strip** the wood and **refinish** it for my daughter Melanie. The **headboard** was **full of scratches**.

Just before starting to take the paint off, I noticed that one of the scratches was a date: September 18, 1946, the day my parents were married. Then it struck me—this was the first bed they had as husband and wife!

Right above their **wedding** date was another name and date: "Elizabeth, October 22, 1947."

My mother answered the phone. "Who is Elizabeth," I asked, "and what does October 22, 1947 mean?"

"She's your sister."

I knew Mom had lost a baby, but I never saw this as anything more than a **misfortune** for my parents. **After all**, they went on to have five more children.

"You gave her a name?" I asked.

"Yes. Elizabeth has been watching us from **heaven** for forty-five years. She's as much a part of me as any of you."

"Mom, there are a lot of dates and names I don't **recognize** on the headboard."

"June 8, 1959?" Mom asked.

"Yes. It says 'Sam'."

扫码听
课文B

Note

47

"Sam was a black man who worked for your father at the plant. Your father was fair with everyone, treating those under him with equal respect, no matter what their race or **religion**. But there was a lot of **racial** tension at that time. There was also a union strike and a lot of trouble."

"One night, some **strikers** surrounded your dad before he got to his car. Sam showed up with several friends, and the crowd **dispersed**. No one was hurt. The strike **eventually** ended, but your dad never forgot Sam. He said Sam was an answer to his **prayer**."

"Mom, there are other dates on the headboard. May I come over and talk to you about them?" I **sensed** the headboard was full of stories. I couldn't just strip and **sand** them away.

"I almost stripped away these remarkable stories," I said. "How could you give this headboard to me?"

"Your dad and I **carved** our first date on the headboard the night we married. From then on, it was a **diary** of our life together. When Dad died, our life together was over. But the **memories** never die."

When I told my husband about the headboard, he said, "There's room for a lot more stories."

We moved the bed with the story book headboard into our room. My husband and I have already carved in three dates and names: Barbara, Greg and Jackson. Someday, we'll tell Melanie the stories from her grandparents' lives and the stories from her parents' lives. And someday, the bed will **pass on to** her.

New Words

strip [strɪp] v. to remove all the things from a place and leave it empty 拆除

refinish [riːˈfɪnɪʃ] v. give a new surface 再抛光,修整表面

headboard [ˈhedbɔːd] n. the vertical board at the end of a bed 床头板

scratch [skrætʃ] n. a mark, a cut or an injury made by scratching somebody's skin or the surface of something 划痕,划伤

wedding [ˈwedɪŋ] n. a marriage ceremony, and the meal or party that usually follows it 婚礼,结婚庆典

misfortune [mɪsˈfɔːtʃən] n. something unpleasant or unlucky that happens to someone 不幸,厄运

heaven [ˈhevn] n. the place believed to be the home of God where good people go when they die 天堂,天国

recognize [ˈrekəgnaɪz] v. to know who somebody is or what something is when you see or hear them, because you have seen or heard them before 认识,辨别出

religion [rɪˈlɪdʒən] n. the belief in the existence of a god or gods, and the activities that are connected with the worship of them 宗教,宗教信仰

racial ['reɪʃl] adj. happening or existing between people of different races 种族的,种族间的

striker ['straɪkə(r)] n. a worker who has stopped working because of a disagreement over pay or conditions 罢工者

disperse [dɪ'spɜːs] v. to move apart and go away in different directions; to make somebody/something do this 驱散,分散

eventually [ɪ'ventʃuəli] adv. at the end of a period of time or a series of events 最后,最终

prayer [preər] n. words which you say to God giving thanks or asking for help 祈祷

sense [sens] v. to become aware of something even though you cannot see it, hear it, etc. 感觉到,意识到

sand [sænd] v. to make something smooth by rubbing it with sandpaper or a sander 用砂纸打磨

carve [kɑːv] v. to write something on a surface by cutting into it 刻

diary ['daɪəri] n. a daily written record of (usually personal) experiences and observations 日记

memory ['meməri] n. a thought of something that you remember from the past 回忆

Phrases

be full of 充满……

after all 毕竟

pass on to 传递给……

Task 8 Fill in the blanks with the words given below and change the word forms if necessary

1. I was _____ (notice) by the traffic police to pay some fine for illegal parking.

2. Happy _____ (married) always comes from mutual help, respect and understanding between a husband and a wife.

3. As the Chinese proverb goes, _____ (fortune) never comes singly.

4. Since these words were inscribed on the stone tablet several hundred years ago, they are almost beyond _____ (recognize).

5. For _____ (religion) reasons, these temples are forbidden to young girls.

6. Everyone is supposed to enjoy equal right in the election regardless of his or her gender, color skin, and _____ (racial).

7. The strikers were _____ (disperse) by the police with tear gas.

8. Such kind of thing will _____ (event) happen if we don't keep alert.

9. Don't be _____ (sense) to his words. He's just kidding.

10. Many English learners find it difficult to _____ (memory) new words and phrases.

Task 9 Choose the correct answer according to the passage

1. What does the story tell us from the beginning to the end? _____

A. The happy marriage between the writer's father and mother in the past years

B. How the writer and her husband handled a piece of furniture her mother gave them

C. What the headboard of an old bed told the writer about the moments of the family

D. It took the writer a lot of time to find someone to fix the headboard of the bed

2. What did the date of September 18, 1946 see in the family? _____

A. The writer's parents got married at that time

B. The parents gave birth to the writer

49

C. The date when the writer got or lost a sister

D. The writer's father got some help from his employer

3. How did Sam help the writer's father when he was in trouble? _____

A. He worked hard with other workers in his father's plant

B. He asked some people to stop the strike

C. When some strikers gathered around the writer's father he went there to help

D. Sam changed his religious belief to stop the racial tension in the plant

4. What did the writer do when she found the dates on the headboard of the bed? _____

A. She managed to get rid of the marks to make the headboard clean and tidy

B. After she sensed all the family stories on it, she sold it

C. She wanted to strip away the stories and gave the bed to her story

D. She and her husband decided to do what their parents did on the headboard

5. What did the writer's mother compare the things on the headboard to? _____

A. dates   B. diary   C. race   D. room

Part 4　Practice and Learn

Participle(分词)

分词由动词变化而来,具有动词和形容词的特征。分词具有形容词功能,同时又表现出各种动词性特点,如时态、语态、带状语性修饰语的性能及带宾语的性能。分词分为现在分词和过去分词两种,是一种非谓语动词形式。现在分词和过去分词的主要差别在于现在分词表示"主动或进行",过去分词表示"被动或完成"。分词可以有自己的状语、宾语或逻辑主语等。

分词有各种类型,如现在分词有一般式 doing、一般被动式 being done、完成式 having done、完成被动式 having been done 等。分词的所有否定式是在分词前面加 not。分词的用法简要介绍如下。

1. 作状语

分词在句子中作状语,可以表示时间、条件、原因、结果、让步、方式、伴随等。分词(短语)作状语时,其逻辑主语应与句中主语相一致。当现在分词表示的动作发生在谓语动词之前时,用现在分词的完成式。当所表示动作与谓语动作同时发生时,用现在分词的一般式。完成或被动关系用过去分词。

The students went out of the library, **smiling and talking.**

Escorted by his friend, he went to the police station.

Given more care, the pets could grow better.

2. 作定语

分词作定语时,单个的分词通常放在被修饰的名词之前;分词短语作定语时,置于被修饰的名词的后面。现在分词修饰发出该动作的名词,过去分词修饰承受该动作的名词。

This is really a **rewarding** day to all of us!

After a night **spent** in excitement and sleeplessness, I forced myself to take a long walk along the beach the next day.

3. 作宾语补足语

现在分词在 see、watch、hear、observe、notice、feel、find、glimpse、glance 等感官动词和 look at、listen to 等短语动词以及使役动词 have 后面,与名词或代词构成复合宾语,作宾语补足语的成分,有三种形式,即动词原形、现在分词和过去分词。其中动词原形表示主动和完成,现在分词表示主动或正在进行,过去分词表示被动或完成。

The gardener found the flowers **picked** up by somebody.

We are watching the performer **doing** his job.

4. 作表语

分词作表语通常当作形容词来用。现在分词表示主语的性质，而且主语多为物；过去分词表示主语的感受或状态，主语多为人。

The situation is **discouraging**.

They are quite **convinced** with the evidence.

Task 10 Choose the right answer based on the grammar rules you learn

1. When they get back home, they found the room _____.
   A. rob   B. to be robed   C. robbed   D. robbing

2. _____ with the best students, I still have a long way to go.
   A. Having compared   B. To compare   C. Compared   D. Compare

3. The music of the film _____ by him sounds so _____.
   A. playing, exciting   B. played, excited   C. playing, excited   D. played, exciting

4. _____ against the coming hurricane, they didn't dare leave home.
   A. Warned   B. Having warned   C. To warn   D. Warn

5. In _____ countries, you can't always make yourself _____ by speaking English.
   A. English-speaking, understand   B. English-spoken, understand
   C. English-speaking, understood   D. English-spoken, understood

6. _____, Tom jumped into the river and had a good time in it.
   A. Be a good swimmer   B. Being a good swimmer
   C. Having been a good swimmer   D. To be a good swimmer

7. _____ how to read the new words, I often look them up in the dictionary.
   A. Having not known   B. Not to know
   C. Don't know   D. Not knowing

8. As his parent, you shouldn't have your child _____ such a book.
   A. read   B. to read   C. reading   D. be reading

9. When _____ the airport, she waved again and again to us.
   A. leaving   B. to leave   C. leave   D. left

10. Once _____, he threw himself into his work and made every effort to do it well.
    A. restart   B. restarting   C. restarted   D. to restart

Part 5   Write and Learn

A Letter Asking for Help（求助信）

求助信是我们遇到一些自己无法解决的事情时向别人请求帮助的书信。它通常包括自我介绍、写信的目的、陈述请求帮助的内容、希望得到帮助并为此表示感谢。书写求助信时语气要委婉和真诚，切忌使用命令语气，同时要清晰表明请求帮助的具体内容。英文求助信常用以下表达。

1. I am writing this letter to ask you for help.
2. I am writing to you to do me a favor.
3. I wonder if you can help me/give me a hand with this.

4. Faced with this problem, I am anxious to get your help.

5. I really appreciate it if you could help me.

6. I have a problem which disturbs me a lot.

【Sample】

假定你是 Mary,你的汽车坏了,维修费太贵,为了省钱,你想求助你的朋友 Mike 帮忙修理。请用英文写一封求助信。

Dear Mike,

　　As you know, my car had been broken down recently. I took it to the mechanic and he said that it was in dire need of a repair; however, it would cost almost ＄500 to get all of the work done. He said that if I had a friend who was knowledgeable about it, it would probably be worth buying the parts myself and having them help.

　　So, I'm writing because I know that you are very handy and enjoy helping friends. Would you be willing to let me borrow your tools and help me get my car tuned up? It would really help me out and save me a good amount of money.

　　I would be happy to compensate you for your time and I will, of course, buy all of the necessary parts. Let me know what would be appropriate for compensation. I really appreciate that fact that I can come to you for this. You are a true and great friend.

Sincerely yours,
Mary

Task 11　Try to write a letter asking for help based on the information given below

假定你是张明,最近你要和父母一起参加为期一周的家庭露营活动。请你给你的朋友刘丽用英文写一封 100 个单词左右的电子邮件,请她帮忙照顾你的宠物狗。要求语言表达准确,避免单词拼写和语法错误,尽量使用多种句式。

Unit 6　Sports

Learning Objectives:

To *describe* different kinds of sports in English.

To *understand* the facts about the Winter Olympics based on passage A.

To *improve* the reading speed by scanning passage B.

To *grasp* the grammar rules related to infinitive in English.

To *learn* the writing of an English application letter.

Part 1　Look and Learn

Warming-up: Look at the following pictures, talk about them and then finish Task 1

fencing

soccer

basketball

swimming

gymnastics

volleyball

New Words

fencing ['fensɪŋ] n. the sport of fighting with long thin swords 击剑

soccer ['sɒkə(r)] n. a game in which two teams of eleven players try to kick or head a ball into the opponents' goal 足球

basketball ['bɑːskɪtbɔːl] n. a game played by two teams of five players, using a large ball which players try to throw into a high net hanging from a ring 篮球

swimming ['swɪmɪŋ] n. the activity of swimming, especially as a sport or for pleasure 游泳,游泳运动

gymnastics [dʒɪm'næstɪks] n. physical exercises that develop and show the body's strength and ability to move and bend easily 体操

volleyball ['vɒlibɔːl] n. a game in which two teams of six players use their hands to hit a large ball backwards and forwards over a high net while trying not to let the ball touch the ground on their own side 排球

Task 1 Match the words in the left column with the explanations in the right column

1. badminton	A. a game played over a large area of ground using specially shaped sticks to hit a small hard ball into a series of 9 or 18 holes, using as few strokes as possible
2. tennis	B. a game like tennis played by two or four people, usually indoors. Players hit a small light kind of ball, originally with feathers around it across a high net using a racket
3. boxing	C. a game in which two or four players use rackets to hit a ball backwards and forwards across a net on a specially marked court
4. golf	D. a long running race of about 42 kilometres or 26 miles
5. marathon	E. a sport in which two people fight each other with their hands, while wearing very large thick gloves

Part 2 Speak and Learn

Task 2 Complete the conversation with the following expressions

A. back and forth
B. butterfly stroke

C. swim cap

D. laps

E. bathing suit

Alisa: Good afternoon, I'm Alisa.

James: I'm James.

Alisa: James, are you ready for the pool?

James: Oh yeah, I've got my 1. _____, my goggles...

Alisa: This cap is funny. How do you use it?

James: It's my 2. _____.

Alisa: It looks weird.

James: It keeps the dirt out of my hair and makes me swim faster. Will you do some 3. _____?

Alisa: Laps?

James: You know, swimming in the lane 4. _____ a few times for exercise.

Alisa: Oh, if someone swim a trip around and around in the pool, he is doing laps. Swimming lap sounds like too much work. I'd prefer to have some sun-bathing.

James: So what is your favorite swimming style?

Alisa: I like breaststroke.

James: Breaststroke is not bad, but I think you could look at my 5. _____.

Alisa: Butterfly stroke is awesome!

James: Have a look!

Alisa: Is that a butterfly? You look like a grasshopper more than a butterfly!

James: Oh, I do not seem like a grasshopper. Will you just comment? Why not come into the pool?

Alisa: Alright, I'm on my way.

Task 3 Answer the following questions according to the dialogue in no more than 3 words

1. Where does this conversation take place?

   This conversation takes place _____.

2. When does this conversation take place?

   It's about _____.

3. What has James got for swimming?

   He has got _____ and goggles.

4. What is Alisa's favorite swimming style?

   She likes _____.

5. What is the function of swim cap?

   It keeps the _____ out of one's hair and makes one swim faster.

Task 4 Talk with your partners about your preparing steps for swimming with the help of the following expressions

1. use the right arm movement...

2. handle the dolphin kick...

3. move your body in a wave-like fashion...

4. you should know the time to breathe...

5. combine them all together...

Part 3　Read and Learn

Passage A

The White Olympics

The Winter **Olympic** Games is a major international sporting event that occurs once every four years. Unlike the Summer Olympic Games, the Winter Olympic Games **features** sports practiced on snow and ice. The first Winter Olympic Games, also known as the 1924 Winter Olympics, was held in Chamonix, France. The Winter Olympic Games was held every four years from 1924 until 1936, after which it was **interrupted** by World War Ⅱ. The Winter Olympic Games was **resumed** in 1948 and was again held every four years. Until 1992, the Winter and Summer Olympic Games were held in the same year.

The Winter Olympic Games is also called the **White Olympics**. At this time, many colorful **stamps** are published to mark the great games. The first stamps marking the opening came out on January 25, 1932 in the United States for the 3rd Winter Olympic Games. From then on, **publishing** stamps during the Winter Olympic Games became a **rule**.

During the 4th Winter Olympic Games, a group of stamps were published in Germany in November 1936. **The five rings of Olympics** were drawn on the front of the **sportswear**. It was the first time that the rings appeared on the stamps of the Winter Olympic Games.

In the 1950s, this kind of stamps became more colorful. When the Winter Olympic Games came, the **host countries** as well as the non-host countries published stamps to mark those games. China also published four stamps in February 1980, when the Chinese **sportsmen** began to take part in the Winter Olympic Games.

Japan is one of the Asian countries that have ever **held** the Winter **Olympic Games**. Altogether 14,500 million stamps were sold to **raise** money for this sports meet.

Different kinds of sports were drawn on these small stamps. People can enjoy the beauty of the wonderful movements of some sportsmen.

Unit 6 Sports

New Words

Olympic [əˈlɪmpɪk] adj. relating to the Olympic Games 奥林匹克的

feature [ˈfiːtʃə(r)] v. to include a particular person or thing as a special feature 使有特色

interrupt [ˌɪntəˈrʌpt] v. to stop something for a short time 使暂停，使中断

resume [rɪˈzjuːm] v. if you resume an activity or if it resumes, it begins again 重新开始

stamp [stæmp] n. a small piece of paper with a design on it that you buy and stick on an envelope or a package before you post it 邮票，标志

publish [ˈpʌblɪʃ] v. to produce a book, magazine, CD-ROM, etc., and sell it to the public 出版，发行

rule [ruːl] n. a statement of what may, must or must not be done in a particular situation or when playing a game 规则，规章

sportswear [ˈspɔːtsweə(r)] n. clothes that are worn for playing sports, or in informal situations 运动服装

sportsman [ˈspɔːtsmən] n. a person who takes part in sport, especially somebody who is very good at it 运动员

hold [həʊld] v. to carry something; to have somebody/something in your hands, arms, etc. 拿住，握住

raise [reɪz] v. to increase the amount or level of something 增加

Phrases

White Olympics 白色奥运会

the five rings of Olympics 奥运五环

host country 东道国

Task 5 Fill in the blanks with the words given below and change the word forms if necessary

1. He has probably said goodbye to his last chance of _____(Olympic) gold.
2. The _____(sportsman) are determined to be a credit to their country.
3. We post up a set of _____(rule) for the house.
4. It was _____(publish) in the "Annals of Internal Medicine".
5. Two incidents in recent days have _____(raise) the level of concern.
6. He has been collecting _____(stamp) since he was eight.
7. Participants should be dressed in appropriate _____(sportswear) and bring their own tennis rackets.
8. After the war he _____(resume) his duties at Emmanuel College.
9. The game was _____(interrupt) several times by rain.
10. The festival will _____(feature) pyrotechnics, live music, and sculptures.

Task 6 Choose the correct answer according to the passage

1. The White Olympics and the Winter Olympic Games _____.
   A. are the same thing   B. are different games
   C. are not held in winter   D. are held in summer
2. The world made it a rule to publish stamps to mark the great world games _____.
   A. after the year 1936   B. after the 3rd Winter Olympic Games

C. before the 3rd Winter Olympic Games   D. before the year 1932

3. The Winter Olympic Games are held once _____.

A. every two years   B. every three years

C. every four years   D. every five years

4. Which of the following is true? _____

A. Only the host countries can publish stamps to mark the Winter Olympic Games

B. Only the non-host countries can publish stamps to mark the Winter Olympic Games

C. All the countries can publish stamps to mark the Winter Olympic Games

D. Japan can't publish stamps to mark the Winter Olympic Games

5. What may appear on the stamps of the White Olympics? _____

A. basketball   B. table tennis   C. football   D. skating

Task 7   Translate the following sentences into Chinese

1. Large supplemental doses of vitamin E can slightly raise blood pressure.

_____

2. Barcelona was chosen to be host of the 1992 Olympic Games.

_____

3. It's the rule of life that everything you have always wanted comes the very second you stop looking for it.

_____

4. The German Sports Federation said it would hold an investigation.

_____

5. Businessmen often invite famous sportsmen to appear in advertisements.

_____

Passage B

Jesse Owens

James **Cleveland** Owens was the son of a farmer and the grandson of black **slaves**. His family moved to Cleveland when he was nine. There, a school teacher asked his name.

"J. C." he **replied**.

She thought he had said "Jesse", so he had a new name.

Owens ran his **first race** at age 13. After high school, he went to **Ohio State University**. He had to work part-time so as to pay for his education. As a **second-year student**, in the Big Ten games in 1935, he set even more records than he would in the Olympic Games a year later.

A week before the Big Ten meet, Owens **accidentally** fell down a **flight of stairs**. His **back** hurt so much that he could not exercise all week, and he had to be helped in and out of the car that drove him to the meet. He **refused** to listen to the suggestions that he give up and said he would try, **event** by event. He did try, and the results are in the record book.

The stage was set for Owens' victory at the Olympic Games in Berlin the next year, and his success would come to be **regarded** as not only **athletic** but also **political**. Hitler did not **congratulate** any of the **African American** winners.

"It was all right with me." he said years later. "I didn't go to Berlin to shake hands with him, anyway."

Having returned from Berlin, he received no telephone call from the president of his own country,

Unit 6   Sports

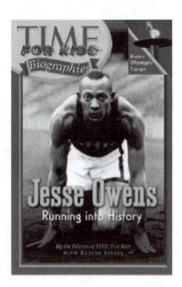

either. In fact, he was not **honored** by the United States until 1976, four years before his death.

Owens's Olympic victories made little difference to him. He earned his living by looking after a school playground, and accepted money to race against cars, trucks, motorcycles and dogs.

"Sure, it bothered me." he said later. "But at least it was an honest living. I had to eat."

In time, however, his gold medals changed his life. "They have kept me alive over the years." he once said. "Time has stood still for me. That golden moment dies hard."

New Words

Cleveland [ˈkliːvlənd] n. the largest city in Ohio; located in northeastern Ohio on Lake Erie; a major Great Lakes port in US 克利夫兰(美国城市)

slave [sleɪv] n. someone who is the property of another person and has to work for that person 奴隶

reply [rɪˈplaɪ] v. to say or write something as an answer to somebody/something 回答, 答复

accidentally [ˌæksɪˈdentəli] adv. an accidental event happens by chance or as the result of an accident, and is not deliberately intended 偶然地, 意外地

back [bæk] n. a person's or animal's back is the part of their body between their head and their legs that is on the opposite side to their chest and stomach 背部, 后背

refuse [rɪˈfjuːz] v. to say that you will not do something that somebody has asked you to do 拒绝

event [ɪˈvent] n. a thing that happens, especially something important 事件, 大事

regard [rɪˈɡɑːd] v. to think about somebody/something in a particular way 认为, 视为

athletic [æθˈletɪk] adj. connected with sports such as running, jumping and throwing 运动员的, 运动的

political [pəˈlɪtɪkl] adj. connected with the state, government or public affairs 政治的

congratulate [kənˈɡrætʃuleɪt] v. to tell somebody that you are pleased about their success or achievements 向(某人)道贺, 祝贺

honor [ˈɒnə(r)] v. bestow honor or rewards upon 给予荣誉

Phrases

the first race 第一名
Ohio State University 俄亥俄州立大学

second-year student 大二年级学生

flight of stairs 阶梯

African American 非裔美籍人

Task 8 Fill in the blanks with the words given below and change the word forms if necessary

1. Early _____ (slave) were generally denied education, but Wheatley was allowed by her owner to study poetry, Latin and the Bible.

2. The senator _____ (reply) that he was not in a position to comment.

3. The damage couldn't have been caused _____ (accidentally).

4. I felt a sharp pain in my lower _____ (back).

5. She _____ (refuse) to accept that there was a problem.

6. A solo piper opens Aberdeen Highland Games at 10:00 a.m. and the main _____ (event) start at 1:00 p.m.

7. He remained the most popular _____ (political) in France.

8. She is widely _____ (regard) as the current leader's natural successor.

9. The authors are to be _____ (congratulate) on producing such a clear and authoritative work.

10. Would you _____ (honor) me by dining with me tonight?

Task 9 Choose the correct answer according to the passage

1. Where is the birthplace of Owens? _____
   A. Cleveland   B. Ohio State   C. Berlin   D. Africa

2. Owens got his other name "Jesse" when _____.
   A. he went to Ohio State University
   B. his teacher made fun of him
   C. his teacher took "J.C." for "Jesse"
   D. he won gold medals in the Big Ten meet

3. In the Big Ten meet, Owens _____.
   A. hurt himself in the back
   B. succeeded in setting many records
   C. tried every sports event but failed
   D. had to give up some events

4. When Owens said "They have kept me alive over the years" in the last paragraph, he means that the medals _____.
   A. have been changed for money to help him live on
   B. have made him famous in the US
   C. have encouraged him to overcome difficulties in life
   D. have kept him busy with all kinds of jobs

5. What would be the best title for the text? _____
   A. Jesse Owens—a great American sportsman
   B. Golden moment a lifetime memory
   C. Making a living as a sportsman
   D. Why was Jesse Owens successful?

Part 4　Practice and Learn

Infinitive(动词不定式)

1. 动词不定式的基本形式

动词不定式的基本形式是"to＋动词原形",有时可以不带 to。动词不定式(或不定式短语)没有人称和数的变化,在句子中不能作谓语。动词不定式仍可保留动词的特点,如可以有自己的宾语和状语。不定式中的动词同它的宾语或状语构成不定式短语,如 to read the newspaper、to speak at the meeting 等。

2. 动词不定式的特征和作用

动词不定式具有名词、形容词和副词的特征,因此在句中可以作主语、表语、宾语、宾语补足语、定语和状语(表 6-1)。

表 6-1　动词不定式的作用及举例

作　用	例　句
作宾语	She wanted to borrow my radio. They began to read and write.
作状语	She went to see her grandma last Sunday. He came to give us a talk yesterday.
作宾语补足语	Lucy asked him to turn off the radio. She asked me to speak more loudly.
作定语	Have you got anything to say? I had something to eat this morning.
作主语	To learn a foreign language is not easy.

需注意的是,作主语用的动词不定式常常用 it 替代,动词不定式(或短语)放在后面。

It is not easy to learn a foreign language.

It took us three days to do the work.

3. 动词不定式的否定形式

动词不定式的否定形式由"not＋动词不定式"构成。

Tell him not to be late.

The policeman told the boys not to play in the street.

4. 不定式省去 to 的情况

在感官动词 see、watch、look at、hear、listen to、feel 和使役动词 make、have、let 等所接的宾语中(不定式作宾语补足语),不定式应省去 to。但是在被动语态中不能省。

Let me listen to you sing the song.

He watched his son play computer games.

I saw him run away. → He was seen to run away.

The boss makes the workers work the whole night. → The workers were made to work the whole night.

5. 动词不定式和疑问词连用

动词不定式可以和疑问词 what、which、how、where、when 等连用,构成不定式短语。

The question is when to start.

I don't know where to go.

He showed me how to use a computer.

What to do is a big problem.

Task 10　Choose the correct answer

1. Tell him _____ the light.
   A. to turn　　　　　B. not to turn on　　C. to not turn　　D. not to turn

2. It took us more than two hours _____ the dinner.
   A. prepare　　　　　B. preparing　　　　C. to prepare　　　D. to be prepared

3. The teacher had his students _____ the desks to make room for a party.
   A. move　　　　　　B. moving　　　　　C. to move　　　　D. be moved

4. The students were made _____ the text ten times.
   A. read　　　　　　B. reading　　　　　C. to read　　　　D. to be read

5. The chair looks rather hard _____, but in fact it is very comfortable.
   A. to sit　　　　　B. to sit on　　　　C. sitting　　　　D. sit

6. Nobody knows _____ next.
   A. what to do　　　B. to do what　　　　C. which to do　　D. how to do

7. It is very important _____ us _____ these words.
   A. to, to remember　　B. for, to remember
   C. for, remember　　　D. for, remembering

8. _____ English well, one must have a lot of practice.
   A. For speaking　　B. Speaking　　　　C. To speak　　　D. Speak

9. I'm going to the library _____ the books.
   A. return　　　　　B. borrow　　　　　C. to return　　　D. to lend

10. We went to town _____ some shopping.
    A. doing　　　　　B. did　　　　　　　C. to make　　　　D. to do

Part 5　Write and Learn

An Application Letter(求职信)

求职信是十分实用的一种应用文。第一段直奔主题说明写信目的,即求职,以及所求职位;第二段为中心段,说明求职条件,即所学专业和最后学历,以及工作经历,包括兼职或做过的工作;结尾段要求面试,盼望回信,写清楚联系方式,并表示感谢。

【Sample】

假定你是李明,某报社招聘新闻信件的编辑,你写信求职。

1. 你毕业于四川大学新闻专业,硕士学位。

2. 你曾担任校报体育编辑;现为华西出版社写稿,并担任编辑。

Dear personnel manager,

　　I notice your ad for a newsletter editor in the October 29 *China Daily*. Because writing and publication work have long been interests of mine, I wish to apply for this position.

　　I believe that both my education and work experience qualify me for the job. In 2011, I graduated from Sichuan University; at the same time, I earned my master degree with a major in Journalism and a minor in English. While in school, I was the sports editor on the campus newspaper. Since graduation, I have written and edited the monthly bulletin of the Huaxi Press.

I am currently available for an interview any weekday after 3:00 p.m. You can reach me at my home phone, 855-7382, and any day after 3:00 p.m. I'm looking forward to hearing from you and appreciate your consideration of my application.

Sincerely yours,
Li Ming

Task 11　Try to write an application letter based on the information given below

假定你是王璐，某医学院护理专业大四学生，即将毕业，某医院正在招聘护士，请写一封求职信。

Unit 7 Travel

Learning Objectives:

To **perfect** oral English by mimicking the conversation.

To **talk about** traveling in fluent and accurate English.

To **improve** reading skills by reading through passage A and passage B.

To **grasp** the basic grammar rules related to gerund.

To **fill in** application forms correctly by imitating the samples.

Part 1 Look and Learn

Warming-up: Look at the following pictures, talk about them and then finish Task 1

luggage

vehicle

accommodation

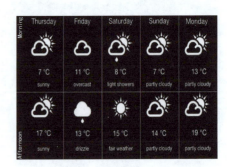

weather

Unit 7　Travel

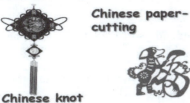

souvenir

tourist attraction

New Words

luggage ['lʌgɪdʒ] n. cases, bags, etc. that contain belongings when they are traveling 行李

vehicle ['viːɪkl] n. things that are used to carry people or goods from one place to another, such as a car or a bus 交通工具

accommodation [əˌkɒməˈdeɪʃn] n. places for living or stay, often also providing food or other services 住宿，住所

weather ['weðə(r)] n. the condition of the atmosphere at a particular place and time 天气

Task 1　Match the words in the left column with the corresponding examples in the right column

1. souvenir	A. storm
2. luggage	B. the Eiffel Tower
3. vehicle	C. five-star hotel
4. accommodation	D. suitcase
5. weather	E. silk scarf
6. tourist attraction	F. bullet train

Task 2　Brainstorming: Work in groups to write out words about travel as many as you can

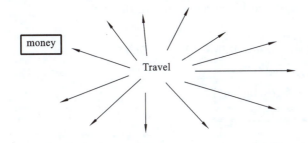

Part 2　Speak and Learn

Task 3　Complete the conversation with the following expressions

A. How long will you stay there

B. The same to you

C. How is everything going

D. do you have any plans for the holiday

E. That sounds tempting

(Two best friends are talking about their plans for the coming summer vacation.)

Rose: Hi, Richard. 1._____?

Richard: So far so good. However, the term is coming to an end, so I have to finish some exams in the next two weeks, which is tough for me. How about you?

Rose: Although there is no exam for me, I have supposed to finish two papers before the end of this month. By the way, 2._____?

Richard: Yes. My parents and I intend to visit Beijing to relax and have fun.

Rose: Wow, so… so… wonderful! Beijing is the capital of China with a great many famous tourist attractions, such as the Great Wall and the Summer Palace. It is really meaningful to have tour there. 3._____?

Richard: Approximately two weeks. Then, maybe we will travel to Thailand. Well, Rose, what's your plan?

Rose: I eagerly look forward to this vacation because I decide to fly to Hawaii and learn sailing for a month. You know, I have been deeply fascinated by that since I was a child. Besides, my uncle lives there, so I can stay in his house and save much money.

Richard: 4._____! You are quick-minded, and can master it soon.

Rose: I hope so.

Richard: Look, I'd better go, or I'll be late for the next class.

Rose: Fine, see you then, and have a good luck.

Richard: 5._____.

Task 4 Answer the following questions according to the dialogue in no more than 3 words

1. What will Richard have to do in the next two weeks?

    Richard will have to _____.

2. By the end of this mouth, what must Rose finish?

    Rose must finish _____.

3. How long will Richard and his parents stay in Beijing?

    They will stay _____.

4. What has Rose been interested in for a long time?

    Rose has been interested in _____.

5. How will Rose travel to Hawaii?

    Rose will _____.

Task 5 Talk with your partners about your plans for the next holiday with the help of the following expressions

1. How is everything going?

2. So far so good.

3. How about you?

4. Do you have any plans for the holiday?

5. What's your plan?

6. How long will you stay there?

7. I eagerly look forward to this vacation.

8. That sounds tempting.

9. Have a good luck.
10. The same to you.

Part 3　Read and Learn

Passage A

The Mountain City—Chongqing

Chongqing, a **metropolis** of more than 30 million people in Southwest China, is **different from** some other Chinese cities.

In 1997, it became the fourth **municipality** of China after Beijing, Shanghai and Tianjin. But many people are drawn to Chongqing by its delicious food and natural scenery. The city looks **futuristic** with its **skyscrapers**, while at the same time, with some 3,000 years of history, it still preserves local culture and lifestyles.

Largely built on mountains and surrounded by the Yangtze and Jialing rivers, it is often called the mountain or river city. After building more than 4,500 bridges in recent years, the largest number in China, it is also **referred** to as the "city of bridges".

After the popular TV **documentary** *A Bite of China* introduced Chongqing noodles and hotpot to the audience **at home and abroad** six years ago, the two **spicy** local **delicacies** have become very popular. Restaurants in many Chinese cities are selling such noodles and hotpot, though people in northern and coastal regions **tend to** eat less chili.

Boasting the largest number of hotpot restaurants in the whole country, Chongqing was named "China's hotpot city" by the China **Cuisine** Association in 2007.

According to the Chongqing Hotpot Association, there are more than 50,000 hotpot **eateries**, employing at least 3.5 million people.

Natural hot springs are a hidden **gem** of the city, where some of the world's oldest hot springs are said to be located. Nowadays, **thanks to** ample **geothermal** resources and its beautiful landscape, Chongqing has developed **dozens of** hot spring spots across the city.

The best seasons to visit Chongqing are spring and fall. The city has long been one of the hottest cities in China due to its **geographical** features and summer temperatures there can **cross** 40 degrees.

New Words

metropolis [mɪˈtrɒpəlɪs] n. a large important city in a country or region 大都会，大城市

municipality [mjuːˌnɪsɪˈpælətɪ] n. a city, town or district with its own government 自治市，直辖市

futuristic [ˌfjuːtʃəˈrɪstɪk] adj. extremely modern and unusual, as if coming from the future 极具现代的，未来派的

skyscraper [ˈskaɪˌskreɪpə(r)] n. very tall modern buildings in a city 摩天楼

refer [rɪˈfɜː(r)] v. to mention or speak about someone or something 提到，谈及

documentary [ˌdɒkjʊˈmentrɪ] n. television or radio programmes, or films, recording facts about something 纪录片

spicy [ˈspaɪsɪ] adj. food having a strong taste with spices in it 辛辣的

delicacy [ˈdelɪkəsɪ] n. a kind of food considered to be very nice to eat 美味佳肴

boast [bəʊst] v. to have something that is impressive and that you can be proud of 拥有

cuisine [kwɪˈziːn] n. a style of cooking 烹饪

eatery [ˈiːtərɪ] n. restaurants or other places serving food 餐馆，饭店

gem [dʒem] n. a precious stone that has been cut and polished and is used in jewelry 宝石，珍宝

geothermal [ˌdʒiːəʊˈθɜːml] adj. relating to the heat in the interior of the earth 地热的

geographical [ˌdʒɪəˈɡræfɪkl] adj. relating to the study of the earth's surface 地理学的

cross [krɒs] v. beyond a limit or boundary 超过，超出

Phrases

be different from 不同于……

at home and abroad 国内外

tend to 倾向于

thanks to 由于

dozens of 几十

Task 6 Fill in the blanks with the words given below and change the word forms if necessary

1. Japanese _____ (different) from Chinese in many aspects.
2. The fantastic scenery in this national park _____ (draw) visitors from all over the country.
3. This precious painting has been well _____ (preserve) in the museum.
4. Mike always _____ (refer) to my nephew as his best friend.
5. This successful company has _____ (boast) many advanced technologies.
6. That famous international company has over 10,000 _____ (employ).
7. The rescue team has successfully _____ (locate) the missing hikers.
8. The animals in this national park have been _____ (ample) protected by the local government.
9. That high school student prefers _____ (geographic) to chemistry.
10. Unexpectedly, he _____ (cross) the line and broke the traffic rule.

Unit 7　Travel

Task 7　Choose the correct answer according to the passage

1. How many people are there in Chongqing according to the text? _____
   A. 300 thousand　　　　　　　　B. over 30 million
   C. less than 30 million　　　　　D. not clear

2. Why is Chongqing often called the mountain or river city? _____
   A. It boasts many rivers
   B. It has a famous mountain
   C. It is largely built on mountains and surrounded by two large rivers
   D. It is isolated from outside

3. After being introduced by the popular TV documentary *A Bite of China*, which two local delicacies in Chongqing have become popular? _____
   A. dumplings and noodles
   B. hotpot and roast duck
   C. hotpot and Chongqing noodles
   D. hotpot and toast fish

4. According to the author, what is the hidden gem of Chongqing? _____
   A. tree　　　B. water　　　C. coal　　　D. natural hot spring

5. What are the best seasons to visit Chongqing? _____
   A. spring and fall　　　　　　　B. spring and winter
   C. spring, summer and fall　　　D. summer and winter

Task 8　Translate the following sentences into Chinese

1. Even if those paintings are already out of fashion, they still present a futuristic flavor, which won't fade soon.

_____

2. Generally speaking, the technique for building a skyscraper, whether at home or abroad, is similar.

_____

3. Many people have been deeply moved by that TV documentary about loneliness.

_____

4. I love to live in a place where I can have a vast variety of cuisines to enjoy.

_____

5. The mountains and woods are typical features of the landscape in Chongqing.

_____

Passage B

Mistakes to Avoid When Visiting a National Park

If you're planning a trip to a national park, here are a few mistakes which tourists often make and you should also know how to avoid them.

Not planning ahead

For any vacation, it's always best to plan ahead. That is especially true for a national park trip. It's best to research your park before going, making sure you've packed **appropriately** for the weather and have all the proper **permits**—especially if you plan on camping or visiting popular attractions. This also gives you an opportunity to **figure out** your **schedule**, so you can **check off** everything on your

扫码听
课文 B

Note

must-see list.

Improperly interacting with wildlife

National parks are perfect places to **spot incredible** wildlife, including **bison**, bears, wolves, big cats and more. However, there is a right and wrong way to **deal with** wildlife and it mostly has to do with giving the animals plenty of space so they don't feel **threatened**.

Not using park maps

Your phone's GPS won't work if you're out of the service area, and some parts of the park might not have a strong **signal**. You'll find some spots that are still connected to outside civilization, but if you're out on the **trails**, you might need to stick to a good and old-fashioned paper map. They most likely can be found in the visitor's center wherever you go.

Going off the trail

While hiking, staying safe should be a top **priority**. The national park service provides a list of items you should always pack for your national park visit, including water, extra food, flashlights, and so on. But one other safety guideline you shouldn't break is going off-trail. Even some experienced hikers can get lost in the national parks, which may lead to injury or even death.

Skipping the visitor center

The visitor center has a **wealth of** knowledge and resources you can **access** about the park you're visiting. Not only is this a good place to find maps, but you can also talk to park **rangers** and get information about special events, closures, and other important details.

Only going during peak season or only visiting the most popular attractions

There are many national parks for every season. Some parks are best visited in the summer, while others are the best in the fall. Even finding a time to go during the off-peak season can be rewarding, especially since this means you likely won't have to **contend** with crowds.

New Words

appropriately [əˈprəʊprɪətlɪ] adv. suitably 适当地

permit [pəˈmɪt] n. an official document which gives someone the right to do something 许可证,特许证

schedule [ˈʃedjuːl] n. a plan that lists all the work that you have to do and when you must do them 日程安排(表)

spot [spɒt] v. to see or notice a person or thing, especially suddenly 发现,认出

incredible [ɪnˈkredəbl] adj. extremely good 极好的，了不起的

bison [ˈbaɪsn] n. a large hairy wild animal of the cow family 野牛

threatened [ˈθretənd] adj. feel as if you are in danger 受到威胁的

signal [ˈsɪɡnəl] n. a sound or movement made to give someone information or instructions 信号

trail [treɪl] n. a route that is followed for a particular purpose 路线，路径

priority [praɪˈɒrəti] n. something that you think is more important than other things and should be dealt with first 优先事项，最重要的事

skip [skɪp] v. to leave out something 遗漏，略过

access [ˈækses] v. to reach, enter or use something 到达，使用

ranger [ˈreɪndʒə(r)] n. a person who takes care of a forest, a park or an area of countryside 护林员

peak [piːk] adj. used to describe the highest level of something, or a time when the greatest number of people are doing something or using something 高峰的，高峰期的

contend [kənˈtend] v. to compete against someone to gain something 竞争，争夺

Phrases

figure out　弄明白，想出
check off　逐一核对
deal with　处理，应付
wealth of　大量的，丰富的

Task 9　Fill in the blanks with the words given below and change the word forms if necessary

1. It is _____ (appropriately) for the president to make a speech right now.
2. Answering phone calls is not _____ (permit) in the library.
3. Finally, I _____ (spot) the difference between the twins.
4. _____ (incredible), my nephew has won the scholarship to study at Yale.
5. The big wild fire was out of control and _____ (threaten) the city.
6. After graduation, finding a job was high on her list of _____ (priority).
7. When you read this book, _____ (skip) any chapters cannot be tolerated.
8. You need a permit to get _____ (access) to these valuable books.
9. We need more hands during the _____ (peak) autumn season.
10. The monkeys in the zoo are _____ (contend) for bananas.

Task 10　Choose the correct answer according to the passage

1. Before having a national park trip, what should you do best? _____
　A. buy a map　　　　　　　　B. research the park
　C. buy camping facilities　　　D. invite someone to travel with you
2. How should you properly deal with wildlife when you are in a national park? _____
　A. feed the animals　　　　　　B. threaten the animals away
　C. give the animals plenty of space　D. ignore the animals
3. What do you need in a national park in case that the GPS on your phone fails to work? _____
　A. a paper map　B. a compass　C. batteries　D. flashlights
4. Which safety guideline do you have to follow when visiting a national park? _____

A. bringing too many things B. bringing nothing
C. traveling alone D. going off-trail

5. What can you do to help yourself in the visitor center beside talking to park rangers and getting information? _____

A. find maps B. have a rest
C. get fresh water to drink D. buy snacks

Part 4 Practice and Learn

Gerund(动名词)

动名词的基本形式为 v-ing,但会随时态和语态的变化而变化。

时态	主动语态	被动语态
一般式	doing	being done
完成式	having done	having been done

动名词的时态就是动名词所表示的动作与句子谓语动词所表示的动作在时间概念上的先后关系；动名词的语态就是动名词的逻辑主语与动名词所表示的动作的关系。

Climbing rocks is a favorite physical activity especially for the youth.（一般式）

Being criticized by the public drove her in an embarrassing situation.（一般被动式）

I am terribly sorry for having brought you much trouble.（完成式）

He was grateful for having been accepted as a member in the association.（完成被动式）

动名词属于非谓语动词中的一类,具有动词的特征和名词的功能。动词的特征即动名词可以带宾语、表语、状语,名词的功能即动名词只能当名词来使用。

Some people are good at remembering numbers.（带宾语）

The locals show great respect to that old man for being generous.（带表语）

Rising early is considered a healthy habit.（带状语）

动名词的否定,即在动名词前加否定副词 not。

Most students fancy not handing in homework.

动名词具有名词的功能,在句子中作主语、宾语、表语、定语。虽然动名词和现在分词的形式一样,皆为 v-ing,但功能却不同,现在分词具有形容词和副词的功能,在句子中作定语、表语、状语、补语。

Seeing is believing.（主语）

The hero risked losing his life to reduce the damage to the minimum.（宾语）

What the child hates most is being punished by his parents.（表语）

When you travel outside, you should take a walking stick.（定语）

Task 11 Choose the correct answer

1. People really enjoy _____ with him because he is always ready to help others.
A. to work B. to have worked C. working D. have working

2. Right now, it's no good _____ about anything.
A. complain B. complaining C. to complain D. having complained

3. That man has been eager for _____ for a long time after he lost his job.
A. employ B. to be employed C. employing D. being employed

4. People know little about her _____ in Britain many years ago.
   A. working   B. worked   C. to work   D. having worked
5. It is very impolite for a person _____ without _____ goodbye.
   A. leave, saying   B. to leave, saying   C. leaving, to say   D. to leave, to say
6. I'll play with you after I finish _____ the house.
   A. to be cleaned   B. to clean
   C. cleaning   D. having cleaned
7. It is really comfortable and pleasant _____ on that chair.
   A. sit   B. to be sitting   C. sitting   D. having sit
8. He still denied _____ to me on that matter.
   A. lying   B. lied   C. to lie   D. having lied
9. I will never forget _____ song sung by that famous star.
   A. to hear   B. to be heard   C. hearing   D. having heard
10. Due to the heavy rain, the president decided to put off _____ the talk.
    A. holding   B. held   C. to hold   D. hold

Part 5　Write and Learn

Application Form（申请表）

如今越来越多的人需要出国留学、参会、旅行等,在此过程中,人们会填写各种各样的表格。其中申请表是最常见也是最典型的表格,因此有必要了解如何正确填写申请表。

【Sample 1】

Application Form

Title：<u>Dr.</u>（Miss/Mr./Mrs./Ms./Dr./Prof.）
Family name (Surname/Last name)：<u>Green</u>
Given name (Forename/First name)：<u>Jerry</u>
Date of birth：<u>15/09/1987</u>（dd/mm/yy）　Gender：<u>Male</u>(Male/Female)
Nationality：<u>American</u>　　　　　　Country of birth：<u>China</u>
Address：<u>No. 30, Hall Street, New York City, New York, USA(85201)</u>
Tel：<u>(403)-7896325</u>　　　　Fax：<u>(403)-7896488</u>
E-mail：<u>Greenny@yahoo.com</u>

【Sample 2】

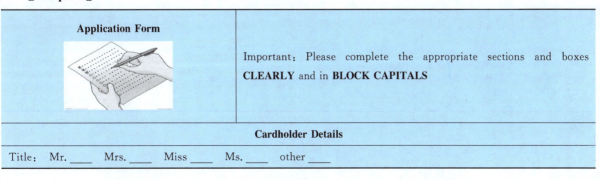

续表

| First name: |
| Surname: |
| Nationality: |
| Address: |
| Telephone: |
| Mobile: |
| E-mail: Postcode: |

Notes on the samples

一般来说,填写申请表相对比较简单,语言简明扼要,主要填写个人信息,按要求完善信息即可,但在填写申请表时须注意以下几个方面的事项。

1. 出生日期(date of birth)有两种写法,即美式(月、日、年(month/day/year))与英式(日、月、年(day/month/year))。

2. 英文地址(address)的写法与中文相反,应按从小到大的顺序写,即门牌号、街道名、城市名、国家名,邮编放到最后。

3. 填写国籍(nationality)时,应填写相应的形容词,如 Chinese,American,Japanese,而非相应的名词。

Task 12　Please write out the corresponding Chinese equivalents for the following commonly-used terms in application forms

1. Full name　　　　_____
2. Christian name　_____
3. Gender　　　　　_____
4. Occupation　　　_____
5. Nationality　　　 _____
6. Marital status　　_____
7. Married　　　　　_____
8. Single　　　　　 _____
9. Home address　　_____
10. Work address　　_____

Task 13　Suppose you will travel overseas next month, now fill out this application form for visa according to your personal information

Surname	First name	Paste recent passport-size photo
Place of birth	Date of birth (Month/Day/Year)	Age	Sex ☐Male ☐Female	

续表

Citizenship	Applicant's address	Telephone No.
Occupation	Business name & address (i.e. company, school, etc.)	

Father's name	Mother's name

| Civil status
☐Single ☐Separated
☐Married ☐Divorced
☐Widowed | If married, name of spouse | Citizenship |
| | Names and ages of children, if any | |

Passport/travel document No.	Date of issue	Valid until	Issued by

Port of entry	Length of stay	Purpose of entry

Destination in the country	

Unit 8 Shopping

Learning Objectives:

To *describe* different kinds of commodities.

To *talk about* online shopping in China and other countries.

To *understand* the main ideas of passage A and passage B.

To *grasp* the basic grammar rules about attribute clauses.

To *imitate* the writing of an online order form.

Part 1 Look and Learn

Warming-up: Look at the following pictures, talk about them and then finish Task 1

foodstuff

clothing

necessities

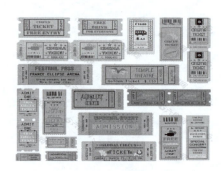

tickets

Unit 8　Shopping

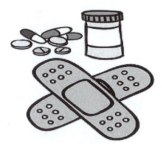

medication

books

New Words

foodstuff [ˈfuːdstʌf] n. any substance that is used as food 食物，食品

necessity [nəˈsesəti] n. a thing that you must have in order to live properly or do something 必需品

medication [ˌmedɪˈkeɪʃn] n. a drug or another form of medicine that you take to prevent or to treat an illness 药品

Task 1　Match the words in the left column with the explanations in the right column

1. food	A. the printed pieces of paper that give you the right to travel on a particular bus, train or go into a theatre
2. clothes	B. the things that you wear, such as trousers/pants, dresses and jackets
3. daily necessities	C. any substance that can be metabolized by an organism to give energy and build tissue
4. tickets	D. a substance used as a medicine or used in a medicine
5. drug	E. products or raw materials needed by people in their daily life
6. books	F. a written work published in printed or electronic form

Part 2　Speak and Learn

Task 2　Complete the conversation with the following expressions

A. not satisfied

B. specified addresses

C. much cheaper

D. online shopping

E. disadvantages

F. the pictures and introduction

Lydia: Hey, Vivian, do you know what is 1. _____?

Vivian: Yeah, sure! I bought a lot of things from the Internet.

Lydia: Really? What did you buy?

Vivian: I have bought some food, such as cookies, kiwi fruit, and two bottles of sparkling water. Aha, I also ordered some clothes which are in French style.

Lydia: Wow, it seems that online shopping is quite convenient.

扫码听
对话

Note

Vivian: Of course! You can choose almost whatever you like!

Lydia: How do you get your goods from them?

Vivian: The websites will deliver your packages to your home or anyplace you want if you have given them 2. _____.

Lydia: Great! So how about the prices?

Vivian: Aha, actually they are 3. _____ than the goods in big shopping malls.

Lydia: It must be quite a smart way for shopping. What are the 4. _____ of online shopping?

Vivian: Um... The biggest problem is that I cannot see the true commodities. I can only look at 5. _____ of them. Sometimes you may get the one that does not fit you.

Lydia: I agree with you. But how can we deal with this kind of situation?

Vivian: You can return them if you are 6. _____. Although some people might think it's troublesome, I do believe online shopping will be a trend in this generation.

Lydia: Thanks a lot for your introduction. It helps a lot! I'll buy some reference books!

Task 3 Answer the following questions according to the dialogue in no more than 3 words

1. What did Vivian buy?

   Vivian bought some _____ and ordered some _____.

2. How can we get goods from the online stores?

   We can get goods from the online stores by _____.

3. How is the price of online commodities compared with that of offline stores?

   It's _____ than offline stores.

4. How can you deal with the goods that you don't like?

   You can _____.

5. What will Lydia buy on the Internet?

   Lydia is going to buy _____.

Task 4 Talk with your partners about your views on online shopping with the help of the following expressions

Advantages:

1. People have generally discovered several advantages in ...

2. ... is playing an increasing important role in people's lives.

3. ... has a positive impact/influence on people's lives.

Disadvantages:

1. In the meantime, we cannot ignore the disadvantages of ...

2. However, the negative aspects of ... are also apparent/obvious/evident.

3. Like anything else, ... also has its shortcomings.

Part 3   Read and Learn

Passage A

I Want to Bring Chinese Online Shopping Home

"China's online shopping makes life easier!" exclaimed Afu, in fluent Chinese mandarin, when talking about how his life was changed by this "great new invention".

Afu, a German coming to China in 2007, is living in Shanghai with his Chinese wife now. Over the past few years, he has **witnessed** the rapid development of China's online shopping.

"Everyone used the Internet, but hardly did they know online shopping." Afu recalled the time when he first came to China. "But now, China's online shopping has been popular by the virtue of goods. These commodities on diverse **platforms** always have **attractive** price, quality and rich variety." he said. "It also draws attention of many foreigners." Afu added, taking Germany, as an example, where online shopping costs long delivery time and **multiple** delivery fees.

According to Afu, in Germany, people usually have to wait three to seven working days to receive the online goods, not to mention non-working days such as weekends and holidays. However, in China, people are used to getting packages on the next day, he noted.

He also mentioned that in addition to delivery fee, in Germany, people have to pay extra fees sometimes, such as insurance fee, service fee, long distance fee, security fee, and **registration** fee. "Whereas in China, the delivery fee is just a few yuan, and sometimes the delivery is even free." Afu said.

China's prosperous online shopping has not only become **indispensable** to Chinese, but also **fascinated** numerous foreign people around the world, who can't help giving the thumbs-up to it.

As the world's largest online retail market for many years, in 2016, China's e-commerce transaction volume reached 26.1 trillion yuan, accounting for 39.2 percent of the global e-commerce retail market.

With the implementation of policies on cross-border e-commerce **pilot** zones and the **unimpeded trade policy** under the **Belt and Road Initiative**, China's online shopping is **bound** to benefit more people like Afu around the world.

New Words

witness ['wɪtnɪs] v. to perceive or be contemporaneous with 见证，目击

platform ['plætfɔːm] n. the combination of a particular computer and a particular operating system 平台

attractive [ə'træktɪv] adj. having power to arouse interest 吸引人的

multiple ['mʌltɪpl] adj. having or involving or consisting of more than one part 多样的，许多的

registration [ˌredʒɪ'streɪʃn] n. the act of enrolling 注册

indispensable [ˌɪndɪs'pensəbl] adj. too important to be without 不可或缺的，必不可少的

fascinate ['fæsɪneɪt] v. to attract or interest somebody very much 使着迷，使神魂颠倒

implementation [ˌɪmplɪmen'teɪʃn] n. the act of accomplishing some aims or executing some orders 实施

pilot ['paɪlət] adj. a pilot plan or a pilot project is one that is used to test an idea before deciding whether to introduce it on a larger scale 试验性的

bound [baʊnd] adj. certain or extremely likely to happen 必然的

Phrases

with the implementation of 随着……的实施
unimpeded trade policy 自由贸易政策
Belt and Road Initiative "一带一路"倡议
be bound to 必然

Task 5 Fill in the blanks with the words given below and change the word forms if necessary

1. Landing in bad weather is a tricky task for any _____(pilot), even the smallest error can lead to disaster.

2. For example, some customers might provide you with _____(multiply) phone numbers or E-mail addresses, while others might not.

3. This is because, even were it not cheap and plentiful, gas would be _____(attract) simply on the grounds of cleanliness.

4. The _____(register) of the university shows an increase of 10 percent over last year.

5. In all cases, you should _____(implementation) and test all changes in your test environment before you consider adding them to your production environment.

6. Anyone who _____(witness) the attack should call the police.

7. Snakes are said to _____(fascinated) small animals.

8. Cars have become a(an) _____(dispensable) part of our lives.

9. You've done so much work—you're _____(bound) to pass the exam.

10. It may interest you to know that a boy answering Rory's description _____(thumb) a ride to Howth.

Task 6 Choose the correct answer according to the passage

1. How much do Chinese people know about online shopping when Afu first came to China in 2007? _____

A. Chinese used online websites to buy commodities frequently in 2007

B. Computers were not commonly seen in China and almost no one knew how to use the Internet

C. Everyone understood how to search online. However, they didn't know much about online shopping

D. It was impossible to buy food, clothes, or books on the Internet due to high rates and some extra fees

2. Why is Chinese online shopping so attractive nowadays? _____

A. Because it charges us lower delivery fees and less extra insurance fees

B. Because many online platforms provide large quantities of cost-effective commodities

C. Because people do not need to wait for a long time

D. All of the above

3. What do we know about German online shopping according to this passage? _____

A. It's not convenient for people in Germany to go shopping online because of late delivery

B. People need to pay many extra fees such as insurance fee, service fee, long distance fee,

security fee, and registration fee

  C. Almost all the German online commodities have higher delivery fees than those on Chinese online platforms

  D. All of the above

 4. When could Chinese people usually get their packages according to this passage? _____

  A. They usually need to wait 3-7 days

  B. They cannot get their goods on weekends or holidays

  C. They can pay extra fees to get their commodities quickly

  D. They can often receive their packages the next day

 5. Which country has the largest online retail market in the world? _____

  A. Germany   B. the United States of America

  C. the China   D. the Great Britain

Task 7 **Translate the following sentences into Chinese**

1. If you have no fixed platform dependencies, I recommend that you try out both and see which one better suits your needs.

2. The plan is to launch a pilot program next summer.

3. This information is never connected with any personal information you supply to us if you register on our website.

4. We're more able than ever to witness the tragedy of millions of our fellow humans on television or online.

5. Of course, these individuals have been around since the beginning of human history and played a more prominent role in some eras than in others.

Passage B

Officials: Majority of Foreign Drugs Sold Online Fake

 China's food and drug **authority** has **announced** a warning about overseas drugs sold online, saying that 75 percent of such drugs are fake. It is issued in the online statement that the reliability of generic anti-cancer drugs sold online cannot have their **authenticity** and quality **guaranteed.** An official investigation shows that 75 percent of foreign **generic** anti-cancer drugs supplied by online agents are fake and ineffective.

 Zhi Xiuyi, a professor of lung cancer diagnosis, said that Chinese cancer patients turn to online agents mainly for cheap generic drugs and foreign new drugs which have not yet been approved in China.

 Due to the high cost of developing new drugs and getting patents, many newly developed drugs are very expensive. However, such drugs are included in the medical insurance systems of the EU and the US, according to Zhi Xiuyi. Most generic drugs which patients commonly see online are made in India, he added.

 Cancer treatments like Gleevec, which typically cost more than 10,000 yuan a month, are not covered by the **domestic medical insurance system**, while the cost for the generic treatments is only about 1,000 yuan a month.

Zhi Xiuyi said that the drugs sold online are risky as they are not be supervised. "Patients can't tell the difference between **genuine** drugs and fake drugs as it requires **technical expertise and equipment**."

Peng Donghong, an official with the drug administration of Shenzhen, said that the online transactions of drug sales have made it difficult to supervise the market. According to Chinese regulations, online drugstores can sell only **nonprescription medicine**, and the stores must obtain authorization from drug authorities.

"In order to keep patients from shifting to generic drugs, Chinese drug authority should quicken the **approval** of foreign drugs into the Chinese market and include more anti-cancer drugs in the healthcare system." Zhi Xiuyi said. It would take several years for the Chinese drug authority to approve any new drug. Meanwhile, the authority should expand the category of anti-cancer drugs covered by healthcare programs to make the drugs more **affordable** for patients.

"It is impossible for the government to absorb the entire cost as the drugs are expensive. Thus, the cost should be shared by three parties: the government, the patient and the drug maker." he said.

New Words

authority [ə'θɒrəti] n. the people or an organization who have the power to make decisions or who have a particular area of responsibility in a country or region 官方,当局

announce [ə'naʊns] v. to tell people something officially, especially about a decision, plans, etc. 宣布,宣告

authenticity [ˌɔːθen'tɪsəti] n. the quality of being genuine or true 真实性,准确性

guarantee [ˌɡærən'tiː] v. something that is a guarantee of something else makes it certain that it will happen or that it is true 保证

generic [dʒɪ'nerɪk] adj. (of a product, especially a drug) not using the name of the company that made it 无厂家商标的,非专利的

genuine ['dʒenjʊɪn] adj. to describe people and things that are exactly what they appear to be, and are not false or an imitation 真正的,非伪造的,名副其实的

approval [ə'pruːvl] n. agreement to, or permission for something, especially a plan or request 批准,通过,认可(计划、要求等)

affordable [ə'fɔːdəbl] adj. if something is affordable, most people have enough money to buy it 价格合理的,多数人买得起的

Phrases

domestic medical insurance system 国内医疗保险系统

technical expertise and equipment 专业技术及设备

nonprescription medicine 非处方药

Task 8 Fill in the blanks with the words given below and change the word forms if necessary

1. Most states _____ (guarantee) the right to free and adequate education.

2. She doesn't _____ (approval) of my leaving school this year.

3. We are willing to _____ (authority) the president to use force if necessary.

4. The doctor offered me a choice of a branded or a _____ (generically) drug.

5. To grow the business, he needs to develop management _____ (expertise) and innovation across his team.

6. We cannot _____ (affordable) any more delays.

7. He made a _____ (genuine) attempt to improve conditions.

8. The government yesterday _____ (announce) to the media plans to create a million new jobs.

9. It's not produced _____ (domestic).

10. She has _____ (authenticity) charm whereas most people simply have nice manners.

Task 9 Choose the correct answer according to the passage

1. According to the report, what's the percentage of drugs sold online counterfeit? _____
  A. 25%   B. 75%   C. 34%   D. 50%

2. Who is Zhi Xiuyi? _____
  A. an official from the drug administration of Shenzhen
  B. a national health minister
  C. a head of national health institution
  D. a professor of lung cancer diagnosis

3. Why are online drugs risky? _____
  A. They are too expensive   B. They are difficult to buy
  C. They are hard to be supervised   D. They are toxic

4. Which kind of drugs could online drugstores sell? _____
  A. drugs of any kind   B. drugs with labels
  C. drugs obtaining authorization   D. drugs prescribed by doctors

5. Who should pay the cost of the drugs for cancers? _____
  A. the government
  B. the individual, drug makers and government
  C. the drug makers
  D. the individual

Part 4　Practice and Learn

Attribute Clause（定语从句）

定语从句是在主从复合句中作定语的句子，以句子修饰和限定名词或代词。定语从句分两类：限制性定语从句和非限制性定语从句。定语从句由关系代词或关系副词引导。

1. 关系代词在限制性定语从句中的作用

(1) 由 who 引导的定语从句，先行词指人，在定语从句中作主语或宾语。

Anybody who breaks the laws will get a penalty.

The tall guy who asked us to hand in the resume worked in the Human Resource Department.

(2) 由 whom 引导的定语从句，先行词指人，在定语从句中作宾语。

The doctor whom you are waiting for has left.

Is she the very person whom we must treat kindly?

(3) 由 whose 引导的定语从句，先行词可指人，也可指物，在定语从句中作主语的定语。

He was the very person whose legs were injured in the accident.

Many mountains whose tops are covered with thick ice and snow all the year are standing at the high altitudes.

(4) 由 which 引导的定语从句，先行词指物，在定语从句中作主语或宾语。

The regional economy which exerts great impact on local industries is the topic being discussed now.

This is the issue which we should take into consideration.

(5) 由 that 引导的定语从句，先行词可以指人或物。

Is oxygen the gas that/which aids fire burning?

2. 关系副词在限制性定语从句中的作用

常见的引导定语从句的关系副词有 when、where、why 等。关系副词在定语从句中作状语，其意义相当于在先行词的前面加相应的介词，以介宾结构作状语。

She could never forget the day when she dated her boyfriend for the first time.

（先行词指时间，when 在从句中作时间状语，相当于 on the day。）

The student union is a warm social place where you can have your competence recognized.

（先行词指地点，where 在从句中作地点状语，相当于 at the place。）

His mother was finding out the reason why he was obsessed with playing games.

（先行词指原因，why 在从句中作原因状语，相当于 for the reason。）

Task 10　Choose the correct answer

1. This is the only one of the students _____ the truth.

　　A. that knows　　B. that know　　C. who know　　D. which know

2. Do you know the girl _____?

　　A. who he often talks　　　　　　B. to who he often talks

　　C. to that he often talks　　　　　D. he often talks to

3. The world _____ we live is made up of matter.

　　A. on which　　B. of which　　C. at which　　D. in which

4. There are no children _____ love their parents.

A. that do not   B. who does not   C. that   D. who

5. The old man _____ yesterday is a scientist.

A. I spoke   B. I spoke to   C. whom I spoke   D. that I spoke to him

6. Abraham Lincoln, _____ led the United States _____ these years, was _____ of the greatest presidents.

A. he, for, a   B. whom, in, one   C. who, at, one   D. who, through, one

7. Who is the girl _____ wears a red dress?

A. whose   B. that   C. whom   D. that's

8. During the days _____, he worked as a servant at the Browns.

A. followed   B. following   C. to follow   D. that followed

9. The young man _____ is an engineer of our factory.

A. that you just talked   B. whom you just talked to
C. which you just talked to   D. who you just talked

10. The dictionary _____ is sold out in the bookshop.

A. you need   B. what you need   C. which you need it   D. that you need it

Part 5   Write and Learn

Order Form（购物订单）

网上购物是近年来最流行的购物模式，而网上购物订单正是每次网上购物消费都会见到的东西。认识各类商品的英文词汇以及学习个人信息的正确填写方式会为国际网上购物提供诸多便利。

【Sample】

Order Form

Commodities	Quantity	Unit price	Total
Shampoo (especially for damaged hair)	1	£15.00	£15.00
Cologne (90 mL)	1	£90.00	£90.00
Eye gel	1	£45.00	£45.00
Facial serum	1	£64.50	£64.50
Total	4	—	£214.50

SUB TOTAL	£214.50
SHIPPING	£5.00
ONLINE DISCOUNT	£−20.00
TAX（0.000%）	£0.00
TOTAL	£199.50

Personal Information

First name	Cynthia	Last name	Waterson
Phone number	15870567034	E-mail	4232890421@icloud.com
Shipping address	House 15 Flat3, Graduate College, the University of Edinburgh, Edinburgh, Scotland, UK		

Postal code   EH1 1JZ

Order confirmation

Task 11 Try to fill in the blanks of a shipping order form based on the information given below

刘源,女

电话:19803237560

电子邮箱:904592349@qq.com

联系地址:中国重庆市江北区建新北路85号

邮编:400000

订单

商品	单价	数量	总价
Harry Potter and the Sorcerer's Stone(《哈利波特与魔法石》)	45元	1	45元
Daisy Dream perfume 小雏菊香水	600元	1	600元
Deep moist hair oil 护发精油	198元	1	198元

Order Form

Commodities	Quantity	Unit price	Total
Harry Potter and the Sorcerer's Stone	1	¥45.00	1. _____
2. _____	1	3. _____	¥600.00
Deep moist hair oil	4. _____	¥198.00	¥198.00
Total	3		5. _____

SUB TOTAL   ¥843.00
SHIPPING   ¥0.00
ONLINE DISCOUNT   ¥0.00
TAX（0.000%）   ¥0.00
TOTAL   ¥843.00

Personal Information

First name	6. _____	Last name	7. _____
Phone number	8. _____	E-mail	9. _____
Shipping address	10. _____		
Postal code	11. _____		

Order confirmation

Unit 9   Psychology

Learning Objectives:

To **describe** people's mental health in English.
To **cultivate** the habit of sticking to a balanced diet according to the conversation.
To **scan** the reading materials to get the main idea of how to keep mental health.
To **grasp** the basic grammar rules related to noun clauses.
To **imitate** the writing of notes and messages.

Part 1   Look and Learn

Warming-up: Look at the following pictures, talk about them and then finish Task 1

positive feeling

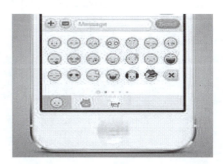
emotion

confidence

negative thinking

depression

stress

New Words

positive ['pɒzətɪv] adj. hopeful and confident, thinking of the good aspects of a situation rather than the bad ones 积极的

mental ['mentl] adj. relating to the state or the health of a person's mind 心理的

emotion [ɪ'məʊʃn] n. a feeling such as happiness, love, fear, anger, or hatred, which can be caused by the situation that you are in or the people you are with 情感

confidence ['kɒnfɪdəns] n. you feel sure about your abilities, qualities, or ideas 信心

negative ['negətɪv] adj. unpleasant, depressing, or harmful 消极的

depression [dɪ'preʃn] n. a mental state in which you are sad and feel that you cannot enjoy anything, because your situation is so difficult and unpleasant 沮丧

stress [stres] n. you feel worried and tense because of difficulties in your life 压力

Task 1 Match the words in the left column with the explanations in the right column

1. definite	A. the part of you that is not physical and that consists of your character and feelings
2. spirit	B. you believe that they are honest and sincere and will not deliberately do anything to harm you
3. mood	C. it is firm and clear, and unlikely to be changed
4. trust	D. the way you are feeling at a particular time
5. pressure	E. force you when you feel hard on something

Part 2 Speak and Learn

Task 2 Complete the conversation with the following expressions

A. heard of

B. pressure

C. Long time no see

D. control my state of mind

E. mental health

Billy: Morning! Ann! 1. _____. How is everything going?

Ann: Everything is all right and now I take exercise every day. By the way, have you 2. _____ Jim these days?

Unit 9　Psychology

Billy: No, I'm busy with my work. What happened?

Ann: He is not as cheerful as usual. I heard last Saturday that his father has been sick. I guess if that's the trouble.

Billy: Maybe he has a problem at work.

Ann: Perhaps. We all have so much 3. _____ from our jobs.

Billy: What we should do is to pay more attention to our 4. _____. Do you think so?

Ann: Ah, right. I paid no attention to this before, and now after hearing your words, I think maybe there is something with me. I often feel uneasy without any reason. Do you know what should I do?

Billy: I don't know. What are you busy with these days?

Ann: I am preparing for an important program.

Billy: You must be too anxious about it. You are worrying about you work, right?

Ann: Yes, kind of. I really hope that I can do the best.

Billy: Just take easy. What you should focus on is the process. If you have prepared very well, the result won't be too bad.

Ann: I hope so. But I can't 5. _____.

Billy: If so, I advise you to ask a psychologist for help soon.

Ann: OK, I will go as soon as possible. We should be aware of mental health regularly. Thanks.

Billy: Don't mention it. May you recover as quickly as possible.

Task 3　Answer the following questions according to the dialogue in no more than 3 words

1. What does Ann do every day?
   She _____ every day.
2. What happened about Jim?
   He is _____ as usual.
3. What do they have to pay more attention about?
   They should pay more attention to _____.
4. What's Ann busy with these days?
   She is preparing for _____.
5. What's Billy's advice to Ann at last ?
   Billy advises Ann to _____ for help soon.

Task 4　Talk with your partners about your opinions about the attention for mental health with the help of the following expressions

1. Long time no see.
2. How is everything going?
3. By the way...
4. What happened...?
5. What we should do is to pay more attention to...
6. What are you busy with these days?
7. May you recover as quickly as possible.

Part 3　Read and Learn

Passage A

A Healthy Mind

Even if some persons feel on top of the world, it's important that they take time to do something for their **inner** well-being. When persons are **mentally** healthy, they're aware of what makes them feel positive and what gets them down. Paying attention to their mental health helps teens to become better equipped to **acknowledge** what they're feeling and to keep a balanced **perspective** on both life and themselves.

Be kind to yourself

People are often kinder to others than they are to themselves. Self-talk is the way people speak to themselves. While people tend to find it easier to believe negative things about themselves, it is important that teens catch any negative self-talk and replace it instead with more positive and **compassionate** thoughts. This will help a person to feel confident and in control.

Build positive relationships

Supportive friends can give persons confidence, and push them to meet their **potential**. Good friends **reinforce** a person's positive thoughts, celebrate each other's achievements, and offer support in hard times, which can be invaluable to a person's inner well-being.

Relax

Whether it's watching a new film, listening to a favorite band, or reading a book, making time for oneself to relax, and it is important for well-being.

Stay active

Exercise releases **endorphins** — the body's natural mood elevator — good for both the body and mind.

Help others

Helping friends and noticing their needs can help people to feel good about themselves and their friendship.

Set goals and ambitions

Having goals **focuses** the mind **on** a task. Staying **on track** and focused when working towards a goal is an important part of building resilience.

Learn new skills

Developing skills outside of a teen's comfort zone can test and develop their **resilience**, as well as give them a chance to meet and become friends with new and different people.

New Words

inner ['ɪnə(r)] adj. the parts contained or enclosed inside the other parts, closest to the center 内心的

mentally ['mentəli] adv. in your mind 心理上

acknowledge [ək'nɒlɪdʒ] v. declare to be true or admit the existence 承认

perspective [pə'spektɪv] n. a way of regarding situations or topics 观点

compassionate [kəm'pæʃənət] adj. feel or show pity, sympathy, and understanding for people who are suffering 有同情心的

potential [pə'tenʃl] n. the necessary abilities or qualities to become successful or useful in the future 潜力,潜能

reinforce [ˌriːɪn'fɔːs] v. make stronger or more intense 加强

endorphin [en'dɔːfɪn] n. a chemical naturally released in the brain to reduce pain 内啡肽

ambition [æm'bɪʃn] n. a strong drive for success 抱负

resilience [rɪ'zɪliəns] n. the ability to recover quickly from difficulties; toughness 恢复力

Phrases

even if 即使

focus on 使……聚焦于

on track 在正道上,未离题(或目标),正轨

Task 5   Fill in the blanks with the words given below and change the word forms if necessary

1. The _____(mental) state that had made her nervous was no longer present.
2. Tea contains caffeine. It's bad for your _____(healthy).
3. The _____(achieve) of these goals will bring lasting peace.
4. His _____(ambition) was to win gold at the Olympic Games in 2016.
5. My father was a deeply _____(compassionate) man.
6. I have a _____(feel) that everything will be all right.
7. I believe that I can deal with the _____(relationship) between playing and learning.
8. China has been stressing the _____(important) of its ties with the third world countries.
9. If you have _____(confident) in someone, you feel that you can trust them.
10. China, as the largest _____(develop) country and a major economy, maintains its own economic stability and development.

Task 6 Choose the correct answer according to the passage

1. What is the way people speak to themselves? _____
   A. telephone
   B. self-talk
   C. talking with friends
   D. not clear

2. Who reinforce a person's positive thoughts, celebrate each other's achievements, and offer support in hard times? _____
   A. parents
   B. classmate
   C. good friends
   D. yourself

3. Which is NOT the way to relax? _____
   A. watching a new film
   B. listening to a favorite band
   C. doing a lot of work paper
   D. reading a book

4. According to the author, what can help people to feel good about themselves and their friendship? _____
   A. laughing at someone
   B. doing house cleaning
   C. making you dreams come true
   D. helping friends and noticing their needs

5. What can test and develop a teen's resilience? _____
   A. developing skills outside of their comfort zone
   B. building positive relationships
   C. being kind to yourself
   D. helping others

Task 7 Translate the following sentences into Chinese

1. Even if some persons feel on top of the world, it's important that they take time to do something for their inner well-being.
   _____

2. People are often kinder to others than they are to themselves.
   _____

3. Supportive friends can give persons confidence, and push them to meet their potential.
   _____

4. Whether it's watching a new film, listening to a favorite band, or reading a book, making time for oneself to relax, and it is important for well-being.
   _____

5. Helping friends and noticing their needs can help people to feel good about themselves and their friendship.
   _____

Passage B

Stress

Whether it's **related to** exams or setback with family, everyone feels stressed sometimes. Stress can be a positive thing, **motivating** teens to work well under pressure, but too much of it can have a harmful effect on a person's emotional and physical health.

Fight or flight

When the body feels stress, it goes into "fight or flight" mode, releasing a mixture of hormones that prepares the body for action. These hormones increase energy, and **divert** blood **away from** the brain and into the muscles. This stress response works well when a person's life is in danger, but it's less helpful when it's **triggered for** something that isn't life-threatening, such as taking an exam.

Signs of stress

People experience stress in different ways, but there are quite a few common **symptoms**. Some people experience these at the same time, such as feeling tired and emotional. Sometimes, one symptom can cause another to happen. The symptoms of stress add to the overall feeling of being stressed by **preventing** people **from** feeling rested and clear-minded, which may make them feel even more stressed.

1. Tiredness

Stress tires out the mind and **muscles**, and can affect sleep, making it harder to **concentrate**.

2. Feeling emotional

Panic attacks and sudden crying are signs of the **acute anxiety** that stress can bring.

3. Anger

Some people become irritable, and angry when stressed.

4. Headaches

Headaches can be a aspect of stress.

5. Chest pains

Chest pains and a rapid and **irregular** heart beat can be triggered by stress.

Dealing with stress

There are no immediate solutions to stress, but there are a number of things that can reduce its effects over time. Though they might seem basic, they can help a person feel calm, rested and supported, and give back a sense of control.

1. Take a break

Try to get some time away from thinking about your problem as it can refresh your **perspective** and **calm** you **down**.

2. Get enough sleep

Though it might be difficult when stressed, a good night's rest is a **massive** factor in overcoming stress and anxiety.

3. Talk

Talking to those around you is a great way of releasing some tension and may help you find solutions to your stress.

4. Exercise

Physical activity not only helps you feel calmer, but also improves the quality of your sleep.

Good and bad stress

Stress can sometimes be very useful, as people have to keep working under pressure and energize them to complete tasks they care about. But if it becomes overwhelming, stress can limit a person's ability to function effectively. When you're feeling stressed, try to use it as a challenge.

New Words

motivate ['məʊtɪveɪt] v. give an incentive for action 激发……的积极性
symptom ['sɪmptəm] n. something wrong with your body or mind that is a sign of the illness 症状
muscle ['mʌsl] n. a piece of tissue inside your body that connects two bones and that you use when you make a movement 肌肉
concentrate ['kɒnsəntreɪt] v. make central 集中
panic ['pænɪk] n. a very strong feeling of anxiety or fear that makes you act without thinking carefully 恐慌
acute [ə'kjuːt] adj. to become severe very quickly but do not last very long 急性的
anxiety [æŋ'zaɪəti] n. a feeling of nervousness or worry 焦虑
irregular [ɪ'reɡjʊlə(r)] adj. occurring at uneven or varying rates or intervals 不规则的
perspective [pə'spektɪv] n. an idea of thinking about something 观点
massive ['mæsɪv] adj. very large in size 非常大的

Phrases

be related to 与……有关
divert...away from 从……转移
trigger for... 为……引发
prevent from 阻止，防止
calm...down (使)平静下来，(使)镇定下来

Task 8 Fill in the blanks with the words given below and change the word forms if necessary

1. He said if his wife's attitude continued to change, he would respond _____(positive).
2. They are _____(motivate) by a need to achieve.
3. Jim _____(pressure) a button and the door closed.
4. Polluted air and water are _____(harm) to people's health.
5. If you are _____(tiredness), you feel that you want to rest or sleep.
6. They provided the management methods and treatment in _____(prevent) from motor damage.
7. The patient is breathing _____(irregular).
8. The _____(anger) man knocked him down.
9. They wish to begin the party _____(immediate) after dinner.
10. The stone lions stand _____(massive) by the side to the Summer Palace.

Task 9 Choose the correct answer according to the passage

1. Which one is NOT the symptom of stress? _____
   A. tiredness   B. happiness   C. feeling emotional   D. chest pains

2. How can you refresh your perspective and calm you down? _____

A. feel calm

B. feel rested and supported

C. try to get some time away from thinking about your problem

D. give back a sense of control

3. According to the author, what is a massive factor in overcoming stress and anxiety? _____

A. a good night's rest	B. a nice friend

C. family	D. sports

4. What is a great way of releasing some tension and may help you find solutions to your stress? _____

A. study	B. shopping

C. traveling	D. talking to people around you

5. Which one of the answers below can help you feel calmer and improve the quality of your sleep? _____

A. physical activity	B. have a rest

C. get fresh air	D. join a party

Part 4　Practice and Learn

Noun Clause(名词性从句)

名词性从句是指在复合句中起到名词作用的从句。由于名词在句子中通常作主语、宾语、表语和同位语，故名词性从句分为四类：主语从句、宾语从句、表语从句和同位语从句。连接代词(who、whom、whose、which、what 等)和连接副词(when、where、why、how 等)都在名词性从句中既保留自己的疑问含义，又起连接作用，充当句子成分。

1. 主语从句

(1) that 引导表示陈述意义的句子作主语从句时，that 绝对不能省。

(2) whether 引导表示一般疑问意义的句子作主语从句。

(3) 连接代词和连接副词(what、which、where 等)引导表示特殊疑问意义的句子作主语从句。

常用 it 代替主语从句作形式主语放于句首，而把主语从句置于句末，调整后的句子更便于阅读和理解。

2. 宾语从句

(1) that 引导表示陈述意义的句子作宾语从句时，that 可以省。

(2) whether、if 引导表示一般疑问意义的句子作宾语从句。

(3) 连接代词和连接副词(what、which、where 等)引导表示特殊疑问意义的句子作宾语从句。

3. 表语从句

(1) that 引导表示陈述意义的句子作表语从句时，that 绝对不能省。

(2) whether 引导表示一般疑问意义的句子作表语从句。

(3) 连接代词和连接副词(what、which、where 等)引导表示特殊疑问意义的句子作表语从句。

4. 同位语从句和定语从句的判定

(1) 看句子功能：定语从句是对先行词进行修饰和限定，同位语从句是对先行词进行解释和说明。

(2) 看先行词：如果先行词为抽象名词，多为同位语从句。

(3) 看句子结构：如果从句句子结构完整，一定是同位语从句；如果从句缺句子成分，一定是定语从句。

(4) 看连词的成分：如果 that 不充当句子成分，一定是同位语从句；如果 that 充当句子成分，一定是定语从句。

Task 10　Choose the correct answer

1. You can only be sure of _____ you have at present; you cannot be sure of something _____ you might get in the future.
   A. that, what　　　B. what, 不填　　　C. which, that　　　D. 不填, that

2. _____ is worth doing at all is worth doing well.
   A. Whatever　　　B. Whoever　　　C. However it　　　D. Whatever it

3. _____ we can't get seems better than _____ we have.
   A. What, what　　　B. What, that　　　C. That, that　　　D. That, what

4. Some people believe _____ is easier for small countries to become strong and rich than for large _____.
   A. that, country　　　B. it, one　　　C. that, countries　　　D. it, ones

5. It is generally considered unwise to give a child _____ he or she wants.
   A. however　　　B. whatever　　　C. whichever　　　D. whenever

6. It was by the roadside _____ the six blind men sat quarrelling about the elephant.
   A. when　　　B. which　　　C. on which　　　D. that

7. Could I speak to _____ is in charge of international sales, please?
   A. anyone　　　B. someone　　　C. whoever　　　D. no matter who

8. Although most of them have no doubt _____ he will pass the exam, I still think there is something about _____ he has really got everything ready.
   A. whether, that　　　B. that, whether　　　C. that, that　　　D. whether, whether

9. Mary wrote an article on _____ the team had failed to win the game.
   A. why　　　B. what　　　C. who　　　D. that

10. Information has been put forward _____ more middle school graduates will be admitted into universities.
    A. while　　　B. that　　　C. when　　　D. as

Part 5　Write and Learn

Notes(留言条)

留言条可以有题目，也可以省略题目。但开篇应有称呼，如果是朋友之间的留言，则称呼可较随便。日期写在右上角，通常只需写星期几或星期几的上午、下午，也可只写上午、下午和具体时间。留言条虽然简单，但是中心一定要突出，要交代清楚事情的时间和地点。

【Sample 1】

Tuesday

Dear Li,

　　As the Spring Festival is coming soon, I'm very glad to invite you to come to a dinner party with several other friends of ours. I'm sure we will have a very happy time and enjoy ourselves. Would you like to come at 5:00 p.m. today, to Room 6 of Changjiang Hotel?

Yours truly,
Sam

【Sample 2】

10:30 a.m.

Dear Ms. Lin,

  Jack called to say that he was terribly sorry because he couldn't attend tomorrow morning's meeting. He will contact you as soon as he comes back.

Lily

Task 11 **Write a note according to the information below**

  范静因为明天举办的讲座而将会议延期至星期三召开,她将此事通知吴小姐,并让吴小姐转告有关人员。

Unit 10 Life

Learning Objectives:

To *describe* your insights about life in English.

To *share* your insights about the epidemic.

To *develop* positive mindsets, values and outlooks about life.

To *grasp* the grammar rules related to inversion in English.

To *learn to write* an English letter of offering advice.

Part 1 Look and Learn

Warming-up: Look at the following pictures, talk about them and then finish Task 1

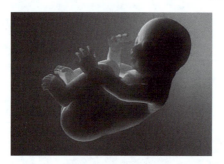

fetus

infant

toddler

preschooler

puberty	senior citizen

New Words

fetus ['fiːtəs] n. an unborn or unhatched vertebrate in the later stages of development showing the main recognizable features of the mature animal 胎，胎儿

infant ['ɪnfənt] n. a baby or very young child 婴儿，幼儿

toddler ['tɒdlə(r)] n. a young child who has only just learned to walk or who still walks unsteadily with small, quick steps 蹒跚行走的人，学步的幼儿

preschooler ['priːˈskuːlə(r)] n. children who are no longer babies but are not yet old enough to go to school 学龄前儿童

puberty ['pjuːbətɪ] n. the time of life when sex glands become functional 青春期

Task 1 Match the words in the left column with the explanations in the right column

1. adulthood	A. the quality of behaving mentally and emotionally like an adult
2. childhood	B. the series of changes that a living thing goes through from the beginning of its life until death
3. juvenile	C. the part of someone's life when they are an adult
4. maturity	D. the part of someone's life when they are a child
5. life cycle	E. relating to a young person who is not yet old enough to be considered as an adult

Part 2   Speak and Learn

Task 2 Complete the conversation with the following expressions

A. are supposed to

B. are addicted to

C. family group photo

D. make different decisions

E. in case of emergency

Steve: Emily, what item will you take or guard 1. _____, say, what is the first thing you will consider to take away from home with you in a fire or an earthquake?

Emily: Are you asking me what is the most important thing in my life?

Steve: Yes. Everybody may 2. _____. A girl once told me that she would take her doll. That amazed me.

扫码听对话

Emily: Not for me! I will definitely take my 3._____. I cherish it all the time. How about you?

Steve: It seems to me that you put your family in the first place in your life. However, I personally believe friendship is one of the best things in my life. I'm lucky to have a lot of supportive and inspiring friends. They make my life so nice and enjoyable.

Emily: Yeah. There are so many things we should value in our life, every place we live, every person we meet, and every tree or flower we see.

Steve: Sure, we should enjoy every single day. I wonder why so many young people 4._____ the virtual life. That looks so unreal.

Emily: I like video games, but I never overindulge in them. I think we should spend more time in real life.

Steve: Maybe in different stages of life we have different things to do. In college life, I personally think the most important thing we 5._____ handle is to get ready for our future life.

Emily: That does make sense. We should be fully prepared for the future, physically, mentally, socially and intellectually.

Steve: Trust me. I really have had a very perceptive talk with you today.

Emily: Me too! I enjoy it!

Task 3 Answer the following questions according to the dialogue in no more than 3 words

1. What will Emily consider in the first place in her life?

   Emily will give priority to her _____ when she makes decisions in life.

2. Which answer to the same question Steve raised amazed Emily?

   Emily felt amazed when someone told her that she would take _____.

3. Why does Steve cherish his friendship?

   Because he thinks that his friends inspire and _____ him all the years.

4. How does Emily like video games?

   She likes them but never _____ in them.

5. According to Emily, in what ways should we get ready for future life?

   She thinks that we should be ready for the future, in _____, social and intellectual ways.

Task 4 Talk with your partners about what is happiness in life with the help of the following expressions

1. a happy reunion after years
2. a long walk with a soulmate friend
3. hear your parents' stories and memories
4. competent and independent when you are away from home
5. a smiley in a text message
6. sing a song with friends using your own lyrics
7. a good talk and a cup of coffee with the person you love
8. being the reason behind your parents' smiles

Part 3　Read and Learn

Passage A

A Great Corrector

Recently someone has **released a message** about what we can learn from the coronavirus **pandemic** sweeping the **globe**. In an open letter, he wrote that he believed that the virus could be a **reminder** to human beings.

It is reminding us that we are all equal, **regardless of** our culture, religion, **occupation**, **financial** situation or how famous we are and that we are all connected and something that affects one person has an effect on another.

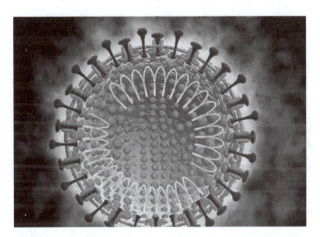

It is **reminding** us **of** how **precious** our health is and how we have moved to **neglect** it through eating **nutrient** poor **manufactured** food and drinking water that is **contaminated** with **chemicals** upon chemicals.

It is reminding us of how important our family and home life is and how much we have neglected this. It is forcing us back into our houses so we can rebuild them into our home and to **strengthen** our family unit.

It is reminding us to **keep** our egos **in check**.

It is reminding us that no matter how great we think we are or how great others think we are, a virus can **bring** our world **to a standstill**.

It is reminding us that this can either be an end or a new beginning. This can be a time of reflection and understanding.

Whereas many **see** the Covid-19 **as** a great disaster, this person prefers to see it as a "great **corrector**". It is sent to remind us of the important lessons that we seem to have forgotten and it **is up to** us if we will learn them or not.

New Words

pandemic [pænˈdemɪk] n. a disease that spreads over a whole country or the whole world（全国或全球性）流行病，大流行病

globe [gləʊb] n. the world (used especially to emphasize its size) 地球，世界

reminder [rɪˈmaɪndə(r)] n. something that makes you think about or remember somebody/

something, that you have forgotten or would like to forget 引起回忆的事，提醒人的事

occupation [ˌɒkjʊˈpeɪʃn] n. a job or profession 工作，职业

financial [fɪˈnænʃl] adj. connected with money and finance 财政的，金融的

precious [ˈpreʃəs] adj. rare and worth a lot of money 珍奇的，珍稀的

neglect [nɪˈɡlekt] v. to not give enough attention to something 忽视，不予重视

nutrient [ˈnjuːtriənt] n. a substance that is needed to keep a living thing alive and to help it to grow 养分，营养物

manufacture [ˌmænjʊˈfæktʃə(r)] v. to make goods in large quantities, using machinery 大量生产，成批制造

contaminate [kənˈtæmɪneɪt] v. to make a substance or place dirty or no longer pure by adding something that is dangerous or carries disease 污染，弄脏

chemical [ˈkemɪkl] n. a substance obtained by or used in a chemical process 化学制品，化学品

strengthen [ˈstreŋθn] v. to become stronger; to make somebody/something stronger 加强，增强

corrector [kəˈrektə] n. someone or something to make something right or accurate 修正者

Phrases

release a message 发布消息

regardless of 不管

remind...of 提醒

keep...in check 控制

bring...to a standstill 使……陷入停顿

see...as 把……看作

be up to somebody 取决于某人

Task 5 Fill in the blanks with the words given below and change the word forms if necessary

1. Urbanization and _____ (globe) are among the current social trends in the 21st century.

2. I use the photo as a _____ (remind) of our long and true friendship.

3. When filling in the blanks in the resume, you have to let them know your previous _____ (occupy).

4. When I am _____ (financial) independent, I will move out from my parents' house and rent a small apartment.

5. The official was blamed for his _____ (neglect) of duty and responsibility.

6. The _____ (manufacture) of drugs should give clear instructions in the labels.

7. The _____ (contaminate) milk was sold and many children suffered for that.

8. He is an outstanding learner in the _____ (chemical) class.

9. The presidents' visit aims to _____ (strength) the bilateral relationship between the two countries.

10. Try to be _____ (reflection) in your learning and that is rewarding.

Task 6 Choose the correct answer according to the passage

1. According to the passage, what did the writer regard the virus as? _____

A. a war　　　　　B. a warning　　　　C. a reminder　　　　D. an accident

2. Where does this piece of writing most probably come from? _____

A. an anonymous letter　　　　　　　　B. a private letter

C. a letter from an ordinary letter   D. a published letter

3. Which statement is true according to the writer? _____

A. A person wanted to tell us his opinion after the outbreak of the virus

B. People are interconnected and something that affects one person doesn't necessary have an effect on another

C. Our culture, religion, and financial situation have an effect on other people

D. The article was written to share the writer's idea with his family

4. How does the writer think of the role of family in our life? _____

A. Our home life is essential to those people who are employed

B. People has paid much attention to and given priority to their family

C. We should do more to construct a better home and make our family stronger

D. Everyone should neglect other things to put family in the first place

5. What does the word "reflection" in the last but one paragraph mean? _____

A. an image   B. imagination   C. a careful thought   D. a sign

Task 7 Translate the following sentences into Chinese

1. We are all born equal, regardless of our culture, religion, occupation and financial situation.

_____

2. This is a friendly reminder. All the passengers please take good care of your personal belongings.

_____

3. Some junk food has been contaminated during the processing, production and delivery process.

_____

4. It is reminding us of how important our lifelong learning is and how much we have neglected it.

_____

5. No matter how powerful a country is, the outbreak of a natural disaster or a nuclear war may bring people's normal life to a standstill.

_____

Passage B

What Keeps Us Healthy and Happy?

We are **constantly** told to **lean into** work, and to **push** harder and **achieve** more. We are given the impression that these are the things that we need to **go after** in order to have a good life. But is that true? Is that really what keeps people happy as they **go through** life?

The Harvard Study of Adult Development may be the longest study of adult life, that's ever been done. For 75 years, they have **tracked** the lives of 724 men. Year after year asking about their work, their home lives, their health, and of course asking all along the way without knowing how their life stories were going to turn out.

The clearest message that we get from this 75-year study is this: good **relationships** keep us happier and healthier. We've learned 3 big lessons about relationships.

The first is that social **connections** are really good for us and that loneliness kills. It **turns out** that people who are more socially connected to family, to friends, and to community are happier. They are physically healthier and they live longer than people who are less well connected.

103

The second big lesson that we learned is that it's not just the number of friends you have, and it's not whether or not you are in a **committed** relationship, but it's the quality of your close relationships that matters. It turns out that living in the midst of **conflicts** is really bad for our health.

And the third big lesson that we learned about relationships on our health is that good relationships don't just protect our bodies, they protect our brains.

What might leaning into relationships even look like? Well, the possibilities are **practically** endless. It might be something as simple as **replacing** screen-time with people-time, or **lightening up** a **stale** relationship by doing something new together, long walks or date nights, or reaching out to that family member who you haven't spoken to in years.

I'd like to close with a **quote** from Mark Twain. More than a century ago, he was looking back on his life, and he wrote this: "there isn't a time, so **brief** his life, for **bickering**, apologies, heart-burnings. There is only time for loving." But **in instant**, so to speak, for that, the good life is built with good relationships. And that's an idea worth spreading.

New Words

constantly [ˈkɒnstəntlɪ] adv. all the time; repeatedly 始终，一直

push [pʊʃ] v. to use your hands, arms or body in order to make somebody/something move forward or away from you; to move part of your body into a particular position 推动（人或物）

achieve [əˈtʃiːv] v. to succeed in reaching a particular goal, status or standard, especially by making an effort for a long time 达到（某种目标、地位、标准）

track [træk] v. to find somebody/something by following the marks, signs, information, etc. that they have left behind them 跟踪，追踪

relationship [rɪˈleɪʃnʃɪp] n. the way in which two people, groups or countries behave towards each other or deal with each other 关系，联系

connection [kəˈnekʃn] n. something that connects two facts, ideas, etc.（两种事实、观念等的）联系，关联

commit [kəˈmɪt] v. to promise sincerely that you will definitely do something, keep to an agreement or arrangement, etc. 承诺，保证

conflict [ˈkɒnflɪkt] n. a situation in which people, groups or countries are involved in a serious disagreement or argument 冲突，争执

practically [ˈpræktɪklɪ] adv. almost; very nearly 几乎，差不多

replace [rɪˈpleɪs] v. to be used instead of somebody/something else; to do something instead of somebody/something else 代替，取代

stale [steɪl] adj. lacking originality or spontaneity; no longer new 陈腐的

quote [kwəʊt] n. a punctuation mark used to attribute the enclosed text to someone else 引文，引语

brief [briːf] v. to give essential information to someone 向……介绍基本情况

bicker [ˈbɪkə(r)] v. to argue about things that are not important （为小事）斗嘴，争吵

Phrases

lean into 倾向
go after 追求
go through 通过
turn out 结果是
lighten up 放轻松，开心一些
in instant 立刻

Task 8 Fill in the blanks with the words given below and change the word forms if necessary

1. _____(constantly) use and practice of English will greatly improve your language skills.
2. We admire the wonderful _____(achieve) they have made in the field of medicine.
3. It takes a person some years to develop from childhood to _____(adult).
4. The _____(relationship) data showed no links between the two things.
5. Many senior citizens in that country live alone and suffer from _____(lonely).
6. _____(physical) inactive lifestyle leads to many potential health problems for human beings.
7. Everything can be _____(possibility) if we strive to make it happen.
8. The machine is _____(practical) useless since it has been broken into pieces.
9. We can see everything clearly in the dark room when it is _____(light) up.
10. I bought some _____(instantly) coffee from that supermarket yesterday.

Task 9 Choose the correct answer according to the passage

1. What is true about the study program mentioned in the passage? _____
A. It lasted more than seven decades
B. It studied the lives of more than one thousand people
C. It studied the work, the family lives, and the income of the people investigated
D. It was sponsored by the federal government of the United States

2. What is the clearest message that we get from this study? _____
A. Economic status is the most crucial factor to be happy
B. Everyone is equally happy regardless of their job, race and marital status
C. Good relationships keep us happier and healthier
D. Family time is the happiest moment for most people

3. According to the passage, which is not true of people more socially connected? _____
A. They are happier   B. They are enjoying a longer life
C. They have healthier body   D. They have better academic performance

4. What is the most important thing according to the study? _____
A. the number of friends that you make   B. a close relationship

C. a committed relationship   D. the quality of the relationship

5. According to the writer, which may not help improve our interpersonal relationship? _____

A. Staying away from TV and get in touch with people

B. Improving a relationship by doing something new together

C. Making more money to make your shopping list longer

D. Reaching out to that family member who you haven't chatted with for a long time

Part 4　Practice and Learn

Inversion(倒装句)

为了强调、突出等目的而颠倒原有语序的句式叫作倒装句。在倒装句中,成分颠倒而句意基本不变,句法成分不变。常见的倒装句句型有以下几类。

1. "there be"结构中,there 是引导词,主语在 be 后。

There are not many people who want to read this book.

2. 疑问句为倒装形式。

Why does he go to school by bike?

3. 在以 so、nor、neither 开头,表示谓语所述的情况也适用于另一个人或事物的肯定或否定句中。so 用于肯定句,表示"也一样""也这样";nor、neither 用于否定句,表示"同样也不""也不这样"。

They didn't manage to do so. Neither did we.

4. 直接引语的全部或一部分放在句首时,主句中的主谓也常倒装。

"May I come in and take a rest?" asked the pool girl.

5. 否定副词开头的句子(部分倒装)。在以 never、hardly、not、only、few、seldom 等否定副词开头的句子中,采用部分倒装;如果不放在句首就不要倒装。

Not until noon did it stop snowing.

6. 以 only 所修饰的副词、介词短语或状语从句的句子。

Only by this means can we hope to succeed.

7. 地点、方位副词在句首(完全倒装)。为了表达生动,有时将表示地点、方位的副词,如 up、down、out、away、in 等放在句首,同时把谓语动词放在主语之前。若主语为人称代词,主语和谓语动词的位置不变,只将副词放在句首。

Out rushed the children.

There he comes.

8. 虚拟结构中,条件从句的谓语含有 were、had 和 should 这三个词时,可省去 if,将这些词移至主语之前。

If I had known, I might have joined the party.

→Had I known, I might have joined the party.

9. so＋形容词、副词及 such 置于句首时。

So strange was his appearance that no one could recognize him.

10. 为了保持句子平衡,或为了强调表语或状语,或使上下文紧密衔接时,可以使用倒装。

They arrived at a house, in front of which sat a small boy.

In a big bed of a big room lies a big man.

Task 10 Choose the right answer based on the grammar rules you learn

1. They had just taken their seats, then _____.
   A. the chairman came   B. the chairman comes
   C. came the chairman   D. comes the chairman

2. _____ so busy, I should come to help you.
   A. Were I not   B. Was I not   C. If I am not   D. If I were not

3. Not until all the fish died in the river _____ how serious pollution was.
   A. did the villagers realize   B. the villagers realize
   C. the villagers did realize   D. didn't the villagers realize

4. Only when I finish my homework _____ watch TV.
   A. I can be allowed to   B. can I be allowed to
   C. I can be allowed   D. can I be allowed

5. On a hill in front of them _____.
   A. stands a great castle   B. a great castle stands
   C. stand a great castle   D. a great castle stand

6. No sooner _____ the telephone rang.
   A. had he got home then   B. he had got home than
   C. had he got home than   D. he had got home then

7. So _____ in the darkness that he didn't dare to move an inch.
   A. he was frightened   B. was he frightened
   C. frightened he was   D. frightened was he

8. Only after I read the text over again _____ its main idea.
   A. that I knew   B. did I know
   C. I could know   D. I did know

9. Little _____ that she was seriously ill herself.
   A. was Susan known   B. knew Susan
   C. did Susan know   D. Susan knew

10. On each side of the street _____ a lot of trees.
    A. are planted   B. is standing   C. plant   D. stands

Part 5 Write and Learn

A Letter Offering Advice(建议信)

建议信是向别人提出合理的建议,让对方接受自己的想法或主张,解决有关问题的信件。建议信不是投诉信(a letter of complaint),给出的观点要合情合理,注意措辞礼貌。建议信通常包括以下内容:说明写信目的;提出建议,列举措施,说明理由等;表示希望对方能够采纳建议。英文建议信常用以下表达法。

1. give somebody advice on/ask somebody for advice/follow one's advice
2. take something into account/consideration
3. I will try to give you some constructive suggestions.
4. In my opinion, it will be beneficial if…/there are many benefits of…
5. I hope that the suggestions will be of great help to you.

6. If you ask me for advice with regard to...
7. Now I am writing to appeal to you to...
8. I think it is high time that we...
9. If we take action now, we will make a difference to...

【Sample】

假定你是 Johnson 的朋友 Peter,他现在是大学最后一年,向你询问选择职业的看法。请你给他写一封建议信,说明你对选择职业的看法和建议。

Dear Johnson,

　　I have received your letter from college and I am glad to know that you are becoming responsible enough to decide on your career.

　　You are now in the final year of college and are about to consider your future job. You know different people may have different priorities in setting a career goal. But all I can say as advice is that you must select a career wisely. The first consideration is your interests. You can only succeed and feel happy when you do something you enjoy. Employment must be both gainful and satisfying. Then you must read up on the latest in the field you are aiming at and acquaint yourself with men and women in profession of that specialization.

Your friend,
Peter

Task 11　Try to write a letter offering advice based on the information given below

假定你是张三,你的美国朋友 Sara 明年将作为志愿者来你校工作。她想提前学习普通话,希望你能给她一些建议。单词数 100 个左右;可以适当增加细节,以使行文连贯。

练习参考答案

Unit 1　College

Suggested keys to the exercises of Unit 1

Task 1
1. B 2. C 3. D 4. E 5. A

Task 2
1. C 2. A 3. D 4. B 5. E

Task 3
1. shows her around 2. students' cafeteria 3. spacious 4. first floor 5. English association

Task 4
(Omitted)

Task 5
1. freedom 2. homesickness 3. adjusting 4. bedding 5. sociable 6. temptation
7. depression 8. purposefully 9. minimize 10. saddened

Task 6
1. C 2. D 3. C 4. D 5. A

Task 7
1. 手机、电脑和平板等电子产品的流行对学生的认知和智力发育产生巨大影响。
2. 你应该保持充足的休息，但不要让自己感到枯燥和厌烦。
3. 应对空气污染的一个办法是通过停止过度使用汽车来减少碳排放。
4. 他是一个无论在哪儿都乐意接受挑战和适应新环境的人。
5. 英语学习的一个方面是很多人忽略的语言技能，如听力和口语。

Task 8
1. jealous 2. scholarship 3. surrounded 4. comprehension 5. adventurous 6. scared
7. expanded 8. confidence 9. natural 10. uncertainty

Task 9
1. A 2. B 3. C 4. D 5. B

Task 10
1. A 2. D 3. A 4. B 5. D 6. D 7. C 8. C 9. D 10. C

Task 11
(Omitted)

Unit 2 Music

Suggested keys to the exercises of Unit 2

Task 1

1. E 2. D 3. A 4. C 5. B

Task 2

1. C 2. E 3. B 4. D 5. A

Task 3

1. classic music

2. on campus

3. its long history

4. The heated atmosphere

5. German music giant

Task 4

(Omitted)

Task 5

1. involvement   2. be distributed   3. regional   4. stimulate   5. evolution

6. ability   7. survived   8. responsibility   9. Emotional   10. functions

Task 6

1. D 2. A 3. B 4. D 5. C

Task 7

1. 只要给予我们更多的时间，我们就一定能找到解决困难的方法。

2. 如果世界人口继续稳定增长，在不久的将来，我们将面临全球人口老龄化的问题。

3. 越来越多的大学生正努力使自己成为对社会和家庭负责的成员。

4. 他频繁缺席讲座，该事实表明他不太专注学习。

5. 警察正在搜寻与该罪犯所犯罪行相关的证据。

Task 8

1. creative   2. challenging   3. findings   4. concluded   5. participate

6. inspiration   7. performed   8. exposed   9. evident   10. theory

Task 9

1. B 2. A 3. C 4. A 5. D

Task 10

1. 主句的谓语，从句的宾语

2. 主语，宾语

3. 主语从句，表语

4. 主句谓语，从句的谓语

5. 形式宾语，真正的宾语

6. 从句的表语，主句的表语

7. 间接宾语，直接宾语

8. 主语，不定式作宾语

9. 主语，宾语

10. 主句的谓语，从句的主语

Task 11

（Omitted）

Unit 3　Health

Suggested keys to the exercises of Unit 3

Task 1

1. B　2. D　3. A　4. E　5. C

Task 2

1. D　2. B　3. A　4. E　5. C

Task 3

1. at home　2. before lunch　3. wash hands　4. turn off　5. properly

Task 4

（Omitted）

Task 5

1. were removed　2. were commanded　3. noble　4. are immune　5. shinier
6. particularly　7. considering　8. be repeated　9. have encouraged　10. gain

Task 6

1. B　2. C　3. D　4. A　5. D

Task 7

1. 即使你最近进行了体检，你还是应该听从医生的建议。
2. 病毒似乎已经伤及他的喉咙和胃。
3. 他衣着华丽，看上去像个贵族。
4. 我对这种病免疫，因为我得过这种病。
5. 很多司机有严重的态度问题。

Task 8

1. healthy　2. confident　3. infection　4. productive　5. afflict
6. frequently　7. irritate　8. have decayed　9. soapy　10. regularly

Task 9

1. C　2. B　3. D　4. C　5. A

Task 10

1. are used　2. is cleaned　3. was stolen　4. will be held　5. going to be given
6. has been lost　7. had been prepared　8. should be looked
9. to be repaired/repairing　10. sells

Task 11

（Omitted）

Unit 4　Food

Suggested keys to the exercises of Unit 4

Task 1

1. E　2. C　3. A　4. B　5. D

Task 2

1. B 2. E 3. A 4. C 5. D

Task 3

1. in a restaurant 2. cauliflower and fruits

3. stewed cabbage 4. fried fish

5. his favorite food

Task 4

(Omitted)

Task 5

1. restrictions 2. allergic 3. particularly 4. harmful 5. microbe

6. suffering 7. asthma 8. immune 9. exposures 10. seeds

Task 6

1. B 2. D 3. A 4. D 5. C

Task 7

1. 并非所有常见于生物中的化学物质都无害。

2. 尽管被曝光后倍感羞耻,他还是重新振作起来了。

3. 为了加快发芽速度,可以把种子在水里浸泡一下。

4. 对猫过敏是哮喘发作最常见的诱因之一。

5. 这一事件表明,他们的领导人免不了会腐败。

Task 8

1. obesity 2. prevention 3. containing 4. risky 5. suffering

6. evolved 7. isolated 8. detection 9. beneficiary 10. Antioxidant

Task 9

1. A 2. D 3. B 4. D 5. C

Task 10

1. C 2. D 3. B 4. A 5. D 6. C 7. A 8. D 9. C 10. C

Task 11

(Omitted)

Unit 5   Family

Suggested keys to the exercises of Unit 5

Task 1

1. E 2. A 3. B 4. C 5. D

Task 2

1. A 2. F 3. B 4. C 5. D 6. E

Task 3

1. southwest China 2. identical 3. new and creative 4. quiet life 5. twice a week

Task 4

(Omitted)

Task 5

1. distancing 2. remarkable 3. arrange 4. impressive 5. Finland 6. dramatically

7. unemployment 8. additives 9. connection 10. Comparatively

Task 6

1. B 2. B 3. C 4. D 5. A

Task 7

1. 在冠状病毒爆发后,这些城市封城并要求居民保持社交距离。

2. 在最近几十年那个国家的人口一直在明显下降。

3. 因为用了讲故事的方法和生动形象的描述,她的演讲给人留下了深刻印象,观众都给她点赞。

4. 那个男孩用钱的数量急剧增加,貌似他想把父母的钱用光。

5. 平均而言,与单身人士相比,已婚人士旅游时间更少。

Task 8

1. notified 2. marriage 3. misfortune 4. recognition 5. religious 6. race 7. dispersed
8. eventually 9. sensitive 10. memorize

Task 9

1. C 2. A 3. C 4. D 5. B

Task 10

1. C 2. C 3. D 4. A 5. C 6. B 7. D 8. A 9. A 10. B

Task 11

(Omitted)

Unit 6 Sports

Suggested keys to the exercises of Unit 6

Task 1

1. B 2. C 3. E 4. A 5. D

Task 2

1. E 2. C 3. D 4. A 5. B

Task 3

1. in the pool 2. afternoon 3. swim cap 4. breaststroke 5. dirt

Task 4

(Omitted)

Task 5

1. Olympic 2. sportsmen 3. rules 4. published 5. raised 6. stamps 7. sportswear
8. resumed 9. interrupted 10. feature

Task 6

1. A 2. B 3. C 4. C 5. D

Task 7

1. 大剂量补充维生素E可能会造成血压偏高。

2. 巴塞罗那获选为1992年奥运会的主办城市。

3. 生活就是这样,你一直想要得到的东西,总会在你不再指望的那一刻姗姗来迟。

4. 德国体育联合会表示将进行调查。

5. 商人们经常请著名的运动员为他们做广告。

113

Task 8

1. slaves   2. replied   3. accidentally   4. back   5. refused   6. events   7. politician
8. regarded   9. congratulated   10. honor

Task 9

1. A   2. C   3. B   4. C   5. A

Task 10

1. B   2. B   3. A   4. C   5. B   6. A   7. B   8. C   9. C   10. D

Task 11

(Omitted)

Unit 7   Travel

Suggested keys to the exercises of Unit 7

Task 1

1. E   2. D   3. F   4. C   5. A   6. B

Task 2

bus, train, credit card, camera...

Task 3

1. C   2. D   3. A   4. E   5. B

Task 4

1. finish some exams   2. two papers   3. approximately two weeks
4. sailing   5. take a flight

Task 5

(Omitted)

Task 6

1. differs   2. draws   3. preserved   4. refers   5. boasted
6. employees   7. located   8. amply   9. geography   10. crossed

Task 7

1. B   2. C   3. C   4. D   5. A

Task 8

1. 虽然那些油画早已过时,但它们仍然呈现了一种未来派的味道,而且那种味道不会很快消退。
2. 一般而言,无论是在国内还是在国外,建造摩天楼的技术是相似的。
3. 很多人被那部关于孤独的电视纪录片深深地感动了。
4. 我喜欢住在一个可以吃很多美味佳肴的地方。
5. 大山和森林是重庆的典型景观。

Task 9

1. appropriate   2. permitted   3. spotted   4. Incredibly   5. threatened
6. priorities   7. skipping   8. access   9. peak   10. contending

Task 10

1. B   2. C   3. A   4. D   5. A

Task 11

1. C   2. B   3. D   4. D   5. B   6. C   7. C   8. D   9. C   10. A

Task 12

1. 全名 2. 教名 3. 性别 4. 职业 5. 国籍
6. 婚姻状况 7. 已婚 8. 单身 9. 家庭住址 10. 工作地址

Task 13

(Omitted)

Unit 8   Shopping

Suggested keys to the exercises of Unit 8

Task 1

1. C 2. B 3. E 4. A 5. D 6. F

Task 2

1. D 2. B 3. C 4. E 5. F 6. A

Task 3

1. food; clothes 2. express 3. much cheaper 4. return them back
5. (some reference) books

Task 4

(Omitted)

Task 5

1. pilot 2. multiple 3. attractive 4. registration 5. implement
6. witnessed 7. fascinate 8. indispensable 9. bound 10. thumbed

Task 6

1. C 2. D 3. D 4. D 5. C

Task 7

1. 如果您没有固定的平台依赖性,我建议您两者都试一下,看看哪一个更适合您的需要。
2. 该计划是在明年夏天实施一个试验性方案。
3. 如果您在我们的网站注册,该信息绝不会与您提供的任何个人信息挂钩。
4. 我们比以往任何时候更有可能在电视或网上看到涉及数百万人的灾难发生。
5. 毫无疑问,这些个体在人类起源之时就存在了,并且它们在某些时代发挥着更突出的角色。

Task 8

1. guarantee 2. approve 3. authorize 4. generic 5. expertise
6. afford 7. genuine 8. announced 9. domestically 10. authentic

Task 9

1. B 2. D 3. C 4. C 5. B

Task 10

1. A 2. D 3. D 4. A 5. B 6. D 7. B 8. D 9. B 10. A

Task 11

1. ¥45.00 2. Daisy Dream perfume 3. ¥600.00 4. 1
5. ¥843.00 6. Yuan 7. Liu 8. 19803237560
9. 904592349@qq.com 10. No. 85 North Jianxin Road, Jiangbei District, Chongqing, China
11. 400000

Unit 9　Psychology

Suggested keys to the exercises of Unit 9
Task 1
1. C　2. A　3. D　4. B　5. E
Task 2
1. C　2. A　3. B　4. E　5. D
Task 3
1. takes exercise
2. not as cheerful
3. mental health
4. an important program
5. ask a psychologist
Task 4
(Omitted)
Task 5
1. mental　2. health　3. achievement　4. ambition　5. compassionate
6. feeling　7. relation　8. importance　9. confidence　10. developing
Task 6
1. B　2. C　3. C　4. D　5. A
Task 7
1. 即使有些人觉得自己处于世界之巅,他们花时间为自己的内心幸福做些事情也是很重要的。
2. 人们通常对他人比对自己更友善。
3. 朋友的支持可以给人信心,并推动他们发挥潜力。
4. 无论是看一部新电影,听一支最喜欢的乐队,还是读一本书,让自己有时间放松,这对幸福很重要。
5. 帮助朋友并注意朋友的需求可以帮助人们对他们自身满意和对这段友谊满意。
Task 8
1. positively　2. motivated　3. pressed　4. harmful　5. tired
6. preventing　7. irregularly　8. angry　9. immediately　10. massively
Task 9
1. B　2. C　3. A　4. D　5. A
Task 10
1. B　2. D　3. A　4. B　5. B　6. D　7. C　8. B　9. A　10. B
Task 11
(Omitted)

Unit 10　Life

Suggested keys to the exercises of Unit 10
Task 1
1. C　2. D　3. E　4. A　5. B

Task 2

1. E 2. D 3. C 4. B 5. A

Task 3

1. family 2. her doll 3. support 4. overindulges 5. physical, mental

Task 4

(Omitted)

Task 5

1. globalization 2. reminder 3. occupation 4. financially 5. negligence 6. manufacturer
7. contaminated 8. chemistry 9. strengthen 10. reflective

Task 6

1. C 2. D 3. A 4. C 5. C

Task 7

1. 无论文化、宗教、职业和经济状况，我们都生而平等。
2. 友情提示，所有乘客请看好自己的个人物品。
3. 一些垃圾食品在加工、生产和运送的过程中被污染。
4. 这提醒我们，终身学习是多么重要，我们是多么忽视这一点。
5. 无论一个国家多么强大，某种自然灾害或一场核战争可能就会让人们的正常生活戛然而止。

Task 8

1. Constant 2. achievement 3. adulthood 4. related/relative 5. loneliness 6. Physically
7. possible 8. practically 9. lightened 10. instant

Task 9

1. A 2. C 3. D 4. D 5. C

Task 10

1. C 2. A 3. A 4. B 5. A 6. C 7. D 8. B 9. C 10. A

Task 11

(Omitted)

参考译文

Unit 1　College

课文 A
大学生活中的想家情绪

大学生活应该是一生中最好的时光。通常对大多数人来说,此言不错。他们远离父母和监护人,享受新获得的自由,结交新朋友,体验新奇的事物。然而,关于上大学,许多人没有提到的一个方面是想家的问题。以下几种实用的办法可以解决大学期间的想家问题。

首先,远离家庭独自生活并不意味着必须努力去适应新环境。如果想更轻松愉快,其实可以带家里的物品到学校宿舍。家庭合照、纪念品和床上用品经常起到很大的作用,让你踏进宿舍房间就有备受欢迎的感觉。

其次,多结交朋友。待在寝室里面、体会你是如何想念家人,这样做对你来说可能是一种诱惑,但是这只能让你的思乡之情越来越深。解决这个问题的一个办法是走出去结识陌生人。结识陌生人会让你找到新朋友,你会和这些朋友分享生活感受,他们也不会让你感到伤心难受。

最后一点,当然并非最次要的一点,是照顾好你自己。避免成天贪睡暴食。你应该要有充足的睡眠,但是不要让自己达到陷入抑郁状态的程度。而且,最好选择健康和均衡的适量饮食,同时安排时间锻炼,以释放激素,让你身心愉悦。

由上可见,想家对许多人来说太正常。给自己足够时间调整,有意让自己忙起来。最重要的是,不要因为想家而觉得惭愧。你一定会克服焦虑,把想家的感觉降到最低。

课文 B
释放失落情绪

当我上大学时,以为一切会很快顺顺当当。我应该就是电影中的那个女孩吧,一开始会很羞涩、紧张,不过很快就会找到同伙和朋友,对一切了如指掌。

因为大学不是电影,所以上面的事情没有发生。我眼睁睁看着同住一楼的女生成了最好的朋友而我的室友和我只是和睦相处而已。我记得当时我嫉妒一个室友,倒不是因为她获得了全额奖学金,而是因为她一到学校就立即有了关系紧密的一群伙伴。

生活在 15 000 位学生中,我感到失落。我就不明白,其他人怎么就这么容易适应大学生活。他们看上去都得心应手,而我到了大学二年级还没能适应。我感觉对我来说已经有点太晚了。

我意识到如果我想要新的经历,我得努力才行。我和学校户外探险社团去冲浪,我还参加了一个志愿者社团,辅导一名五年级的小女孩。每次我冒险做一件新的事情时,总是有点害怕,但是我感觉这是值得的。我认识新人物、尝试新事情,走出舒适区。在大学生活里我对自己越来越有信心。我有些努力是失败了,但是另外一些形成了我的大学经历甚至我的职业生涯。

作为大一新生,在大学里感到失落就像世界末日。回首往事,我很高兴走过了那个阶段。大学里感

118

到失落其实是一件很自然的事情。我已经意识到,其实每个人都会不同程度地有这样的感觉。大学只是生活中一段过渡的时期。当你感到忐忑不安的时候,不应该把这个当成托词故步自封,不去尝试新事物。人们应该接受失落感,把失落感当成一个机会,去探索他们想要的。

我本来可以在大学四年把自己关在寝室,寻思为什么生活总是没有变化。但是我没有,我起身动手,融入校园生活,越做越好。失落感给我带来了动力,它花了我一些时间,但是我没有让它击败自己,我只是利用它使自己的心态变得越来越开放。

Unit 2　Music

课文 A

我们为什么喜欢音乐?

只要我们还有记忆,音乐就一直与我们同在。乐器的发现可以追溯到几万年前。然而,没有人知道我们为什么喜欢音乐,也没有人知道音乐有什么功能。

研究人员尚未在大脑中找到"音乐中心"。与许多高阶过程一样,处理和欣赏音乐所涉及的任务分布在大脑的几个区域。

一项研究发现,受试者集中关注某一个音乐片段的和谐性时,他的右颞叶听觉区域的活动会增强。一些研究表明,颞叶是理解某些音乐特征的关键区域之一。但颞叶与负责形成有意义的音乐结构的额叶的某些区域密切相关。

其他的研究集中在我们对音乐的情感反应上。2001年,麦吉尔大学的一项实验利用大脑扫描来研究音乐有时能诱发鸡皮疙瘩的神经机制。他们发现,被激活的大脑结构区域与食物、性和药物等其他刺激相同。在与奖赏、情感和唤醒相关的区域,大脑中的血液流动随着音乐的起伏而起伏。

正如食物和性的刺激对一个有机体的生存很重要,在人们对音乐特征的反应中可观察到类似的神经活动。该事实表明,进化的一些优势可能会成就人们听或哼一首好曲子的能力。

课文 B

音乐与创造力

从莫扎特到金属乐队 Metallica,很多人在写作或绘画时喜欢听各种类型的音乐。很多人认为音乐有助于提高创造力,但一项由英国和瑞典研究人员进行的国际研究正在挑战这一观念。

兰开斯特大学和中央兰开夏大学的心理学家说,他们的发现表明音乐实际上阻碍了创造力。

为了得出结论,研究人员让参与者在安静的房间里完成旨在激发创造力的语言洞察任务,然后在背景音乐播放的时候再次完成。他们发现,背景音乐"显著削弱"了参与者完成与语言创造力相关的任务的能力。

研究小组还测试了图书馆里常见的背景噪声,但他们发现这些噪声对受试者的创造力没有影响。

这些任务是简单的文字游戏。例如,参与者被提供三个单词,如衣服、表盘和花。然后,他们被要求找到一个与这三个单词相关联的单词,可以组合成一个常见的短语或单词。在本例中,这样一个单词可以是"sun"(太阳裙、日晷、向日葵)。

参与者在一个安静的房间里完成任务,或者在接触三种不同类型的音乐时完成任务:不熟悉歌词的音乐、器乐或熟悉歌词的音乐。

兰开斯特大学的尼尔博士说:"我们发现,与安静的背景条件相比,在播放背景音乐时,人们有明显的表现受损的迹象。"

尼尔博士和他的同事们认为音乐干扰了大脑的语言工作记忆过程,阻碍了创造力。此外,就图书馆背景噪声似乎没有影响而言,研究者认为是这样的,因为图书馆噪声创造了一个"稳定状态"的环境,不会扰乱注意力。

值得一提的是，即使是熟悉的、歌词广为人知的音乐，也会损害参与者的创造力，无论它是否引起积极的反应，或参与者在听音乐时是否在学习或创作。

研究报告写道："总而言之，该发现质疑了人们普遍认为的音乐能增强创造力的观点，相反，它证明了无论是否存在语义内容（没有歌词、熟悉的歌词或不熟悉的歌词），音乐都会持续干扰洞察力问题解决中的创造性表现。"

Unit 3　　Health

课文 A

污垢的前生今世

大多数人认为清除污垢是件好事。然而，人们对污垢的看法并不是一成不变的。

16世纪初，人们认为皮肤上的污垢能阻挡疾病。有医学观点认为，用热水洗去污垢会使皮肤毛孔张开而导致疾病。公共澡堂被认为是一个特别危险的地方。1538年，法国国王关闭了其王国的浴室，随后1546年英国国王也宣令关闭。于是，在很长的一段时间内，欧洲的富人和穷人都与污垢亲密相处。法国国王亨利四世以肮脏著称。他在得知一位贵族洗澡后，下令其不得出门以避免疾病的侵袭。

尽管对污垢优点的信念由来已久，但从18世纪开始，污垢就不再被认为是人们亲密无间的好友。科学地讲，清除污垢对健康有好处。供应洁净水和洗手是预防疾病的有效手段。然而，自二战以来，清洁标准已经超过了科学范畴。广告中反复宣扬这样的理念：衣服要比白色更白，布料要更柔软，表面要更有光泽。对污垢的憎恶是否太过了？

如今，人们对污垢的态度仍然大相径庭。许多初为父母的家长告诫孩子不要接触脏的泥土，他们认为这可能是疾病传播的原因。与之相反，一名美国免疫学家却鼓励孩子们在泥土中玩耍，以建立强大的免疫系统。而这一观点得到了一定的支持。

课文 B

保 持 清 洁

保持日常卫生习惯，除了健康饮食和定期锻炼外，青少年还应该保持身体干净，没有异味。此外，良好的卫生习惯可以促进青少年的心理健康并增强自信。

个人卫生

不良的个人卫生是不健康的，并可能增加感染的风险，所以，青少年尽快养成健康的习惯是最佳选择。

头发

在青春期，毛囊根部皮脂（油）的过量分泌会使头发变得油腻稀疏，或使死皮细胞黏在一起，产生头皮屑。

可定期用少量洗发液洗头并彻底冲洗来避免这些苦恼。有些人每天都需要洗头，而有些人则可以一个星期或更长时间才洗头。

眼睛

触碰眼睛前洗手可以降低结膜炎也就是"红眼病"的风险和其他感染发生风险。尤其是戴隐形眼镜或眼镜的青少年有必要定期去医生那里检查。

皮肤和指甲

皮肤是身体最大的器官，所以保持它的健康是必不可少的。每周去一次角质，可使用温和的磨砂膏去除死皮，但避免过于频繁使用，因为这样可能会导致皮肤干燥和刺激。通过定期保湿保持皮肤水分。可以使用短毛刷清洁指甲和趾甲。

牙齿

为了保持口腔健康,每天至少刷牙齿和牙龈两次。用牙线剔掉牙缝里的食物有助于防止蛀牙。请尽量少吃糖果和含糖饮料。

腋窝

腋窝布满了汗腺。腋窝的温暖环境是细菌分解汗液的理想场所,这也会导致该部位产生异味。

为了尽量减少体味,每天都要用温水和肥皂清洗腋窝。很多人每天使用除味剂以减少出汗并掩盖难闻的气味。

脚

脚底的汗腺比人体表面的任何地方都多,这就是脚底是最臭的部位的原因。

用温热的肥皂水洗脚并彻底擦干,特别是脚趾之间,这能防止真菌感染如脚癣。

Unit 4 Food

课文 A

我们是不是越来越容易对食物过敏了?

我们知道吃太多不合适的食物对我们的健康有害,但是对于有些人来说,食物过敏意味着吃某些东西实际上是有害的——现在看来,这正在影响越来越多的人。

过敏是由免疫系统对抗环境中的物质引起的,这些物质被称为过敏原,它们应该被视为无害的。食物过敏会引起危及生命的反应,这意味着人们不得不终身遵守严格的饮食限制。我们经常听到人们对乳制品和花生过敏。去年,一名15岁的女孩因为吃了含有芝麻的面包而引起致命的过敏反应而死亡。这促使人们呼吁制定更好的食品标签法。

研究发现这个问题对儿童影响更大。伦敦国王学院的亚历山德拉·桑托斯博士在英国BBC网站上写道:"例如,食物过敏现在影响英国大约7%的儿童和澳大利亚9%的儿童。在整个欧洲,2%的成年人有食物过敏"。

那么原因是什么呢?桑托斯博士说过敏发生率的增高不仅仅是因为社会越来越了解过敏且越来越善于诊断过敏,更多的是由于环境的影响。她表示:"可能的因素是污染、饮食变化和接触微生物较少,这些改变了我们的免疫系统的反应"。她指出,对于移居到另一个国家的移民来说,在新的地方患上哮喘和食物过敏是很常见的。

为了找到治愈方法,我们做了很多工作,但这并不容易。所以现在过敏患者必须注意他们的饮食,必须依靠清晰准确的标签。

课文 B

食物和健康

现在,人们患上肥胖症、各种疾病、癌症的概率越来越高。但从另一方面来说,现代药物已发展到一定阶段,即人们可以依赖先进的药品和设备来治疗癌症。

但是,说到治疗癌症,预防和发现可能是防患于未然的最好办法。所以,我们应该找到一些可以早期预防癌症的方法。从另一方面来说,我们也可以摄取健康的食物来预防或者延缓癌症,以下介绍四种对身体有益的食物。

1. 胡萝卜

尽管胡萝卜主要被认为对视力有好处,但过去十年的研究证实,胡萝卜还可以对抗癌症,包括前列腺癌。

在小鼠身上进行的实验发现,摄入胡萝卜可以阻止前列腺癌的生长。胡萝卜还有许多其他的好处,所以吃胡萝卜非常好!

2. 西蓝花

西蓝花是抗癌小能手,可以抵御多种癌症。其中,它们抵抗结肠癌和膀胱癌的作用最好。你可以随便烹饪西蓝花,生吃、凉拌或者做成熟食,它的营养基本不会流失!西蓝花的纤维素含量很高,可以促进肠胃蠕动。所以,多吃西蓝花对身体有好处。

3. 西红柿

西红柿既健康又好吃。煮熟的西红柿可以促使你的身体释放更多的番茄红素,这种植物化学成分对抗癌症的效果特别好。西红柿也有许多抗氧化剂,可以预防和治疗前列腺癌。吃西红柿的方法也有很多。它可以生吃、熟吃,也可以榨汁。

4. 坚果

你想预防乳腺癌或者前列腺癌吗?坚果可以帮助你。它们含有许多ω-3,这种脂肪酸对健康有好处,可以降低我们患冠心病的风险和胆固醇高水平。坚果可以在早饭时吃,也可以作为零食。

Unit 5　Family

课文 A

我们独处的时间更长了吗?

由于冠状病毒的传播,在世界上很多地方,人们被要求甚至被命令保持社交距离。对于我们当中那些独处的人来说,这可能意味着要独处更长时间。

实际上,早在冠状病毒爆发前,人们独处的时间一直在明显延长。不仅独自生活的人如此。单亲父母、丁克一族、三代同堂家庭中的成员独处的时间都越来越长。

一些相关数据令人印象深刻。以下是一份针对芬兰人的研究发现:人们独处的时间急剧延长。没有孩子的单身者独处时间延长最多。总的说来,人们独处的时间随着年龄增长而延长。平均而言,有工作的人比失业的人的独处时间要少一些。

在这份研究中,只有待在一起才算作和他人共处。一个有待回答的问题是人们用电脑的时间有多少算作和他人联系呢。

仅仅从这份研究中,我们无法得知芬兰人独处时间和其他国家的人独处时间的比较。有其他研究比较了儿童独处的时间。如有研究提示,与西班牙和英国儿童比较,芬兰儿童平均每天要多花至少一个小时的时间独处。

课文 B

床头板上的故事

父亲去世几个月后妈妈把床转给我时,这张床约有 45 年的历史了。我决定把它刨一下并重新装饰,给我女儿梅兰睡。床头上全是各种划痕。

正要把漆去掉时,我注意到有一处划痕是一个日期:1946 年 9 月 18 日,我父母结婚的日子。这时我恍然大悟:这是他俩成为夫妻后用的第一张床!

就在他们结婚日期的上方还有一个名字和一个日期:"伊丽莎白,1947 年 10 月 22 日。"

我母亲接的电话。"伊丽莎白是谁?"我问,"1947 年 10 月 22 日又是什么意思?"

"她是你姐姐。"

我知道妈妈失去过一个婴儿,可我以前以为这不过是父母的一件不幸事罢了。何况他们后来又生了五个孩子。

"你们给她起的名字?"

"嗯。伊丽莎白这 45 年一直在天上看着我们。她和你们一样,都是我的一部分。"

"妈妈,床头板上有好多我不明白的日期和姓名。"

"1959年6月8日吗?"妈妈问。

"对,上面写的是'山姆'。"

"山姆是一个在厂里给你爸干活的黑人。你爸待人一视同仁,对手下的人都很尊重,不管他们的种族和宗教信仰如何。不过当时种族关系很紧张。工会还组织了罢工,出了不少事。

"一天夜里,你爸去取车,一些罢工工人在路上把他围住了。山姆和几个朋友赶来,大伙才散了。谁也没伤着。罢工最后结束了,可你爸从此记住了山姆。他说山姆是对他做祷告的回应。"

"妈妈,床头板上还有一些日期。我去跟你谈谈好吗?"我觉察到床头板上有说不尽的故事。我可不能把它们都刨掉蹭掉。

"我差点把这些不平凡的故事刨掉了,"我说,"你怎么能把这床头板给我呢?"

"你爸和我在新婚之夜在床头板上刻下了我们的第一个日期。从那时起,它就成了我们共同生活的记事本。你爸去世了,我们的共同生活就完结了。但是那些记忆永远不会消失。"

我把这块床头板上的故事讲给我丈夫听,他说:"上面有的是空,我们还可以记好多事。"

我们将这块有故事的床头板连床一起搬进了房间。现在,我丈夫和我已经刻上了三个日期和名字:芭芭拉、格雷格和杰克逊。有朝一日,我们要给梅兰讲她外公外婆一生中的故事,讲她爸爸妈妈一生中的故事。终有一天这张床也要传给她。

Unit 6 Sports

课文 A

白色奥运会

冬季奥运会是一项重大的国际体育赛事,每四年举行一次。与夏季奥运会不同,冬季奥运会的特点是在冰雪上比赛运动项目。第一届冬季奥运会,即1924年冬季奥运会,在法国夏慕尼举行。从1924年到1936年,冬季奥运会每四年举行一次,之后被第二次世界大战打断。冬季奥运会于1948年恢复,每四年举行一次。直到1992年,冬季和夏季奥运会在同一年举行。

冬季奥运会也被称为白色奥运会。此时,许多五颜六色的邮票被发行来纪念这些伟大的赛事。标志着奥运会开幕的第一批邮票是于1932年1月25日为了在美国举行的第三届冬季奥运会发行的。从那时起,在冬季奥运会期间发行邮票成了一条规则。

在第四届冬季奥运会期间,即1936年11月在德国发行了一组邮票,奥运五环被印在运动服的前面。这是冬季奥运会邮票上第一次出现奥运五环。

在20世纪50年代,这种邮票变得更加丰富多彩。当冬季奥运会到来时,主办国以及非主办国都会发行邮票来纪念。中国还在1980年2月发行了四种邮票,当时中国运动员开始参加冬季奥运会。

日本是举办过冬季奥运会的亚洲国家。它共售出145亿张邮票,为这次奥运会筹款。

这些小小的邮票上印了不同种类的运动。人们可以欣赏运动员们的精彩时刻。

课文 B

杰西·欧文斯

詹姆斯·克里夫兰·欧文斯是一个农民的儿子、黑人奴隶的孙子。他9岁的时候,他的家迁居到了克利夫兰。在那里,一名学校老师问他叫什么名字。

"J.C.。"他回答说。

她原以为他说的是"杰西",因此他有了一个新的名字。

欧文斯在13岁参加第一场比赛。高中毕业后,他又到美国俄亥俄州立大学。他不得不做兼职工作来支持他上学。作为一名大二年级的学生,在1935年的"十强"运动会上,他创造了比他一年后在奥运会上还要多的纪录。

在那个十强赛的一周前，欧文斯不小心从楼梯上掉下来。他背后的伤使他一个星期不能进行锻炼，为了参赛他甚至不得不需要有人帮助他上、下汽车。他没有听取很多人让他放弃比赛的建议，并表示他将尽全力一项一项地参赛。他做到了，他创造了一项又一项纪录。

第二年的柏林奥运会是欧文斯的舞台。他的成功不仅被认为是竞技的胜利，也是政治上的胜利。希特勒没有向任何一位非裔美国获奖运动员表示祝贺。

"这对我无所谓，"事后几年，他这样说，"我去柏林并不是为了和他握手。"

从柏林返回后，他也没有收到自己国家总统的电话。事实上，直到他去世的四年前，也就是1976年，他才得到美国给予的荣誉。

欧文斯在奥运会上的胜利并没有给他带来任何变化。他靠看护运动场为生，并与汽车、卡车、摩托车和狗赛跑挣钱。

"是的，这让我烦恼，"他后来说，"但至少我过着诚实的生活。我要吃饭。"

终于，他的金牌改变了他的人生。"是这些金牌让我活了下来，"他曾经这样说，"时间在我面前停滞不前。夺取金牌的时刻永远闪亮。"

Unit 7　Travel

课文 A

山城——重庆

重庆位于中国西南地区，是一个人口超过三千万的大城市，它与中国的其他城市不一样。

1997年，重庆成为继北京、上海、天津之后的第四个直辖市，但很多人仍然是被它的美食和风景所吸引。重庆因其摩天楼而具有未来派的感觉。同时，这座拥有三千年历史的城市仍保留着当地的文化和生活方式。

重庆主要建在山上，并且长江和嘉陵江绕城而过，故其常被称为山城或水城。近年来，重庆修建的桥超过了4500座，是中国桥梁数量最多的城市，从而也被称为"桥都"。

六年前，著名电视节目《舌尖上的中国》向国内外的观众介绍了重庆的小面和火锅。自此以后，这两种辛辣的重庆美食受到了大众的欢迎。在中国很多城市的饭店，你都能尝到这两种美食，尽管北方和沿海的人们不喜欢吃辣。

在中国，重庆拥有数量最多的火锅店，2007年被中国烹饪协会命名为"中国火锅之都"。

据重庆火锅协会的统计，重庆火锅店的数量超过了50000家，解决了至少350万人的就业问题。

天然温泉是重庆的一颗隐藏的明珠。据说，一些世界上最古老的温泉位于重庆。如今，因丰富的地热资源和美景，重庆在全市开发了数十个温泉景点。

到重庆游玩的最佳季节是春秋两季。由于独特的地理环境，重庆是中国最热的城市之一，夏季温度能超过40 ℃。

课文 B

游览国家公园时应当避免的错误

如果你计划到一所国家公园游玩，那么你应当知晓如何避免游客经常犯的一些错误。

无计划

对于任何假期，最好要提前做好计划，特别是去国家公园游玩时，提前做计划尤其重要。去玩之前，最好要研究你所游玩的国家公园，尤其当你打算在那里露营或者游览热门景点时，能确保带上应对当地天气所需的物品以及所有的相关许可证。这使得你有机会制定日程安排表，以便一一核查所有想游览的东西。

不文明对待野生动物

国家公园是观看各种神奇的野生动物的最佳地点,如野牛、熊、狼、大型猫科动物等。然而,对待野生动物的方式有正误之分,最好给予野生动物大量的空间,让它们感觉不到威胁。

不使用公园地图

如果你不在服务区,那么你手机的GPS将无法使用,而且国家公园中有些地点的信号也不强。在游玩时,你会发现有些地点依然与外界相连,但是如果你已经在去这些地点的路上了,那么你就可能需要老式的纸质地图。无论你去哪里,纸质地图最有可能在游客中心找到。

偏离路线

在徒步旅行时,安全应当放在第一位。在国家公园里游玩时,国家公园服务中心会提供你所需的一系列物品,包括水、备用食物、手电筒等。但是你还应该遵守另外一条安全指南,即不偏离路线。即便一些经验丰富的徒步旅行者也可能在国家公园里走丢,这可能会导致受伤甚至死亡。

忽略游客中心

在游客中心,你可以找到大量关于你所游览的国家公园的信息和资源。在这里,你不仅可以找到地图,还可以和护林员交谈,了解公园的一些特别之处、关闭的时间以及其他重要的细节。

只在旺季游览或者只游览热门景点

很多国家公园四季都可以游玩。一些国家公园游玩的最佳时间是夏季,而另一些则是秋季。即便在淡季,去国家公园游玩也是挺不错的,特别是此时去游玩的游客不多。

Unit 8　Shopping

课文 A

我要把中国网购带回家

当谈论到网络购物这项伟大的发明是如何改变生活的时候,阿夫操着一口流利的中文如是说:"中国网购真是太方便了!"

阿夫是一位2007年来华的德国人,如今和妻子定居在上海。在过去的这些年里,阿夫见证了"中国网购"的飞速发展。

"每个人都会上网,但是很少有人了解网购。"阿夫回忆起他刚来中国的时候,"但现在,因为商品优质,'中国网购'变得十分受欢迎。这些在不同网络平台出售的商品往往有着吸引人的价格、质量,以及丰富的种类。"他说。"这些商品同样也吸引了众多外国人的目光。"阿夫将德国作为一个例子补充道,在德国网购,不但等待邮寄的时间会花很久,还会被收取各种各样的邮寄费。

据阿夫称,在德国,人们通常需要等待3~7个工作日才能收到网购商品,还不包括像周末或者是节假日这种非工作日。然而在中国,人们已经习惯于第二天就收到包裹了,他提到。

阿夫接着说到邮寄费。在德国,有时人们必须支付额外的费用(例如保险费、服务费、远程运输费、安全费以及注册费等)。但是在中国,邮寄费通常只需要几块钱,有时候甚至是免费的。

发达的"中国网购"不仅是国人不可缺少的一部分,同样也吸引着世界各国众多的外国人,他们都对"中国网购"称赞不绝。多年来中国一直是世界上最大的网络零售商,2016年,中国电子商务交易额达到26.1万亿元,约占全球电子商务零售市场交易总额的39.2%。

随着跨境电子商务试验区政策以及"一带一路"倡议下的自由贸易政策的实施,"中国网购"必将使全世界更多的像阿夫一样的人受益。

课文 B

官方消息:网上出售的进口药大多数是假的

国家食品药品监督管理局发布了一条关于"网售进口药"的警告声明,里面提到75%的"网售进口药"都是假的。这个声明宣布道,网售"非专利抗癌药"不仅真实性不可靠,而且质量也无法得到保障。官方调查显示网络零售商提供的75%的"非专利抗癌药"都是假的,是没有任何效果的。

　　支修益是一位肺癌诊断专家。他说国内癌症患者在网上求购药品的主要原因是因为"非专利药"更便宜,或者是因为可以购买到有些国内未同意生产的"外国新型药"。

　　生产药物及获得专利需要消耗大量的金钱,因此许多最新发明生产的药品十分昂贵。据支修益说,这些新型药是包含在欧盟或者是美国医疗保险系统中的。目前市面上患者常见的大多数"非专利抗癌药"是印度生产的,他补充道。

　　像格列卫这样治疗癌症的药物,通常一个月会花费患者1万元以上,却未包含在国内医疗保险系统中。然而网购"非专利抗癌药",患者一个月仅需花1000元左右。

　　支修益说网购药未被监管,所以它们风险很大。"患者无法区分真药和假药,因为需要专业技术和仪器检测。"

　　一位叫彭冬红的深圳药品监管官员说道:"网上药品交易让市场监管变难了。根据中国的管理条例,线上药店只能够售卖非处方药,并且这些网店都得具备药品监管局的授权。"

　　"为了阻止患者购买'非专利抗癌药',中国不仅应该加快授权外国药品进入中国市场的节奏,还应该在医疗保险系统中增加更多的抗癌药。"支修益说道。国家食品药品监督管理局会花数年时间去授权新药。与此同时,当局应该扩大医疗保险系统抗癌药的种类,应当让患者更有能力支付药品价格。

　　"让政府负担全部的药品支出是不可能的,因为这些药品太昂贵了。药品花费应该由三个部分组成:政府,患者以及药品制造商。"彭冬红说道。

Unit 9　Psychology

课文 A

健 康 心 理

　　即使有些人觉得自己处于世界之巅,他们花时间为自己的内心幸福做些事情也是很重要的。当人们的心理健康时,他们就会知道什么使他感到积极,什么会使他们沮丧。注意青少年的心理健康可以帮助他们更好地了解自己的感受,并对生活和自己保持平衡的心态。

善待自己

　　人们通常对他人比对自己更友善。自我暗示是人们对自己说话。尽管人们往往更容易相信关于自己的消极情绪,但更重要的是,青少年要提防任何消极的自我暗示,代之以更积极和富有同情心的想法。这将帮助一个人感到自信和产生自控力。

建立积极的关系

　　朋友的支持可以给人信心,并推动他们发挥潜力。优秀的朋友可以增进人的积极思想,庆祝彼此的成就,并在困难时期提供支持,这对一个人的内心幸福是无价的。

放松

　　无论是看一部新电影,听一支最喜欢的乐队,还是读一本书,让自己有时间放松,这对幸福很重要。

保持活跃

　　锻炼会释放内啡肽——人体的自然情绪提升剂——对身体和心灵都有好处。

帮助别人

　　帮助朋友并注意朋友的需求可以帮助人们对他们自身满意和对这段友谊满意。

设定目标和抱负

　　有目标会使头脑专注于一项任务。朝着目标前进时保持正确的方向和保持专注,是建立适应能力的重要组成部分。

学习新技能

在青少年的舒适区以外开发新技能可以测试和发展他们的适应能力,并为他们提供机会去遇见不同的人并与这些人成为朋友。

课文 B

压 力

无论是关于考试还是家庭挫折,每个人都会有时感到压力。压力可以是一件积极的事情,激励青少年在压力下良好地工作,但压力过大可能会对人的情绪和身体健康产生有害影响。

应对或逃跑

当身体感到压力时,它会进入"应对或逃跑"模式,释放出各种激素,为身体做好准备。这些激素增加能量,并将血液从大脑转移到肌肉。当人的生命处于危险中时,这种压力响应效果很好,但是如果它触发了对生命没有威胁的事情,例如参加考试,则压力响应就没有多大用处了。

压力的表现形式

人们以不同的方式体验压力,但是有一些常见表现。有些人会同时感觉到疲惫和情绪激动等。有时,一种状态可能导致另一种状态的发生。压力的表现会让人们休息不好,思路不清晰,从而增加整体的压力感,这可能会让他们感到更有压力。

1. 疲倦

压力会使人身心疲惫,影响睡眠,使人难以集中精力。

2. 情绪化

惊恐发作和突然哭泣是压力可能带来的急性焦虑的表现。

3. 愤怒

有些人在感到压力时变得急躁和愤怒。

4. 头痛

头痛可能是压力的一个方面。

5. 胸痛

压力会触发胸痛、快速和不规则的心跳。

应对压力

尚无立即解决压力的方法,但是有很多方法可以随着时间的推移减轻压力的影响。尽管它们看起来很普通,但它们可以帮助一个人感到平静、精力充沛和得到支持,并恢复自我控制。

1. 休息一下

试着在一段时间内不去考虑你所焦虑的问题,因为这样可以更新你的观点并使你平静下来。

2. 充足的睡眠

尽管在压力下可能会很困难,但一夜安眠是克服压力和焦虑的重要因素。

3. 谈话

与周围的人交谈是释放压力的一种好方法,也许可以帮助你找到解决方案。

4. 运动

进行体育锻炼不但可以使你感到镇定,而且可以改善睡眠质量。

压力的益处和坏处

压力有时会非常有用,因为人们必须在压力下持续工作,并激励他们完成其关心的任务。但如果压力过大,压力可能会限制一个人有效工作的能力。当你感到压力时,试着把它当作一种挑战。

Unit 10　Life

课文 A

难得的纠错机会

最近,有人就我们能从肆虐全球的冠状病毒大流行中学到什么发表了一些看法。在一封公开信中他写道,他认为病毒可能是对人类的一种提醒。

病毒提醒我们,人都是平等的,无论我们的文化、宗教、职业、经济状况如何,或是一个人有多么出名。病毒提醒我们,我们的命运都是连在一起的,影响一个人的事情同时也会影响另一个人。

病毒提醒我们,健康多么珍贵。而我们却忽视健康,吃垃圾食品,喝被各种化学品污染的水。

病毒提醒我们,家庭是何等重要,但我们却忽视了这一点。病毒强迫我们回到我们的房子里,所以我们可以把房子重建成家庭,并加强家庭纽带。

病毒提醒我们,我们不能妄自尊大。

病毒提醒我们,无论你觉得自己多伟大,也无论别人觉得你多么伟大,一个小小的病毒就能让整个世界停摆。

病毒提醒我们,疫情既是结束也是开始。我们现在可以反省和理解。

许多人认为新冠病毒的疫情是一场灾难,但这个人觉得这是一次"伟大的纠错"。它让我们重新想起我们似乎已经忘记的重要功课。现在还要不要学习这些功课,完全取决于我们自己。

课文 B

什么让我们健康和开心?

我们总是被告诫要投入工作,努力奋斗,完成更多任务。我们似乎觉得要生活得更好,这些就是我们需要追求的。可事实真是这样吗?这些真的是在人类生命历程中帮助我们保持幸福感的东西吗?

哈佛成人发展研究可能是目前有关成年人生活研究中历时最长的。75 年间,他们追踪了 724 名男性,年复一年地询问这些人的工作、家庭生活、健康状况,当然他们在询问过程中并不知道这些人的人生将会怎样。

我们从这项长达 75 年的研究中得到的最清晰的信息是良好的关系让我们更快乐、更健康。对于关系,我们学到了三条经验。

第一条经验是社会联系真的对我们有益,而孤独是有害的。事实证明,与家庭、朋友和周围人群联系更紧密的人更幸福。他们身体更健康,他们也比联系不甚紧密的人活得更长。

我们学到的第二条经验是起决定作用的不是你拥有的朋友的数量,也不是你是否在一段稳定的亲密关系中,而是你的亲密关系的质量。事实证明,处于冲突之中真的对我们的健康有害。

我们学到的第三条关于关系对我们健康的影响是良好的关系不仅能保护我们的身体,也能保护我们的大脑。

投入一段关系到底是什么样的呢?可能性是无限的。也许是简单到将与屏幕打交道的时间来与人打交道,或者通过一起做些新鲜事,比如散步或者约会,或者联系多年来不曾说过话的家庭成员,来让一段死气沉沉的关系重焕生机。

我想用马克·吐温的一句名言来结束我的演讲。一个多世纪前,当他回顾自己的一生时,他说道:"生命如此短暂,我们没有时间争吵、道歉、伤心。我们只有时间去爱。"所以说,美好的生活是建立在良好的关系上的,而这种理念值得传播。

Glossary

A

access [ˈækses] v. to reach, enter or use something 到达,使用 　　U7P3B

accidentally [ˌæksɪˈdentəli] adv. an accidental event happens by chance or as the result of an accident, and is not deliberately intended 偶然地,意外地 　　U6P3B

accommodation [əˌkɒməˈdeɪʃn] n. places for living or stay, often also providing food or other services 住宿,住所 　　U7P1

achieve [əˈtʃiːv] v. to succeed in reaching a particular goal, status or standard, especially by making an effort for a long time 达到(某种目标、地位、标准) 　　U10P3B

acknowledge [əkˈnɒlɪdʒ] v. declare to be true or admit the existence 承认 　　U9P3A

activate [ˈæktɪveɪt] v. make something more active 激活 　　U2P3A

acute [əˈkjuːt] adj. to become severe very quickly but do not last very long 急性 　　U9P3B

additional [əˈdɪʃənl] adj. more than first mentioned or usual 附加的,额外的 　　U5P3A

affliction [əˈflɪkʃn] n. (formal) pain and suffering or something that causes it 折磨 　　U3P3B

affordable [əˈfɔːdəbl] adj. if something is affordable, most people have enough money to buy it 价格合理的,多数人买得起的 　　U8P3B

allergic [əˈlɜːdʒɪk] adj. characterized or caused by allergy 过敏的 　　U4P3A

allergy [ˈælədʒi] n. hypersensitivity reaction to a particular allergen 过敏 　　U4P3A

ambition [æmˈbɪʃn] n. a strong drive for success 抱负 　　U9P3A

ample [ˈæmpl] adj. enough or more than enough 足够的,丰裕的 　　U1P3A

amplifier [ˈæmplɪfaɪə] n. an electronic equipment to strengthen signals 扩音器,放大器 　　U2P1

announce [əˈnaʊns] v. to tell people something officially, especially about a decision, plans, etc. 宣布,宣告 　　U8P3B

antioxidant [ˌæntiˈɒksɪd(ə)nt] n. substance that inhibits oxidation 抗氧化剂 　　U4P3B

anxiety [æŋˈzaɪəti] n. a feeling of nervousness or worry 焦虑 　　U9P3B

appropriately [əˈprəʊpriətli] adv. suitably 适当地 　　U7P3B

approval [əˈpruːvl] n. agreement to, or permission for something, especially a plan or request 批准,通过,认可(计划、要求等) 　　U8P3B

arousal [əˈraʊzl] n. a state of heightened physiological activity 觉醒 　　U2P3A

arrangement [əˈreɪndʒmənt] n. a plan or preparation which you make so that something will happen or be possible 安排,准备 　　U5P3A

asthma [ˈæsmə] n. respiratory disorder characterized by wheezing 气喘,哮喘 　　U4P3A

athletic [æθˈletɪk] adj. connected with sports such as running, jumping and throwing 运动员的,运动的 　　U6P3B

attack [əˈtæk] v. to use violence to try to hurt or kill somebody 袭击,攻击 　　U3P3A

attitude [ˈætɪtjuːd] n. the way that you think and feel about it 态度 　　U3P3A

129

attractive [əˈtræktɪv] adj. having power to arouse interest 吸引人的   U8P3A
auditory [ˈɔːdɪt(ə)ri] adj. relating to the process of hearing 听觉的   U2P3A
authenticity [ˌɔːθenˈtɪsəti] n. the quality of being genuine or true 真实性，准确性   U8P3B
authority [əˈθɒrəti] n. the people or an organization who have the power to make decisions or who have a particular area of responsibility in a country or region 官方，当局   U8P3B
average [ˈævərɪdʒ] n. a level which is usual 平均水平，一般水准   U5P3A

adjust to 调整   U1P3A
African American 非裔美籍人   U6P3B
after all 毕竟   U5P3B
as far as... 就……而言   U2P3B
as/so long as... 只要……   U2P3A
at home and abroad 国内外   U7P3A

B

back [bæk] n. a person's or animal's back is the part of their body between their head and their legs that is on the opposite side to their chest and stomach 背部，后脊   U6P3B
backdrop [ˈbækdrɒp] n. scenery hung at the back of stage 背景   U2P1
balcony [ˈbælkəni] n. a platform that is built on the upstairs outside wall of a building, with a wall or railing around it 阳台   U5P1
basketball [ˈbɑːskɪtbɔːl] n. a game played by two teams of five players, using a large ball which players try to throw into a high net hanging from a ring 篮球   U6P1
bedroom [ˈbedrʊm] n. a room for sleeping in 卧室   U5P1
bicker [ˈbɪkə(r)] v. to argue about things that are not important （为小事）斗嘴，争吵   U10P3B
bison [ˈbaɪsn] n. a large hairy wild animal of the cow family 野牛   U7P3A
boost [buːst] v. increase or be beneficial to something 提高   U2P3B
bound [baʊnd] adj. certain or extremely likely to happen 必然的   U8P3A
brief [briːf] v. to give essential information to someone 向……介绍基本情况   U10P3B
broccoli [ˈbrɒkəli] n. a plant with dense clusters of tight green flower buds 西蓝花   U4P3B

be amicable with 与……友好相处   U1P3B
be aware of 意识到   U4P3A
be bad for 对……不利   U4P3A
be beneficial for 对……有益   U4P3B
be bound to 必然   U8P3A
be designed to... 旨在   U2P3B
be different from 不同于……   U7P3A
be exposed to... 暴露在……面前   U2P3B
be full of 充满……   U5P3B
be good for 有益于，对……有好处   U3P3A
be harmful 对……有害   U4P3A
be jealous of 嫉妒……   U1P3B
be limited to 限于   U3P3B
be related to 与……有关   U9P3B

be responsible for... 对……负责 U2P3A
be up to 取决于某人 U10P3A
Belt and Road Initiative "一带一路"倡议 U8P3A
bond with 结合 U1P3B
bring . . . to a standstill ……陷入停顿 U10P3A

C

cafeteria [ˌkæfɪˈtɪərɪə] n. a restaurant where you choose and pay for your meal at a counter and carry it to a table. 自助餐厅 U1P1
callings [ˈkɔːlɪŋz] n. a strong desire or feeling of duty to do a particular job, especially one in which you help other people 强烈愿望 U10P3B
carve [kɑːv] v. to write something on a surface by cutting into it 刻 U5P3B
chemical [ˈkemɪkl] n. a substance obtained by or used in a chemical process 化学制品, 化学品 U10P3A
chicken [ˈtʃɪkɪn] n. the flesh of a chicken used for food 鸡, 鸡肉 U4P1
cholesterol [kəˈlestərɒl] n. an animal sterol normally synthesized by the liver 胆固醇 U4P3B
classroom [ˈklɑːsrʊm] n. a room in a school where lessons take place 教室 U1P1
Cleveland [ˈkliːvlənd] n. the largest city in Ohio; located in northeastern Ohio on Lake Erie; a major Great Lakes port in US 克利夫兰（美国城市） U6P3B
colleague [ˈkɒliːɡ] n. the workmate 同事 U2P3B
colon [ˈkəʊlən] n. the part of the intestine between the cecum and the rectum 结肠 U4P3B
command [kəˈmɑːnd] v. to tell somebody to do something 命令 U3P3A
commit [kəˈmɪt] v. to promise sincerely that you will definitely do something, keep to an agreement or arrangement, etc. 承诺, 保证 U10P3B
compassionate [kəmˈpæʃənət] adj. feel or show pity, sympathy, and understanding for people who are suffering 有同情心的 U9P3A
comprehend [ˌkɒmprɪˈhend] v. to understand something fully 理解, 领悟 U1P3B
concentration [ˌkɒnsənˈtreɪʃən] n. the action of focusing on something 集中, 专注 U2P3B
confidence [ˈkɒnfɪdəns] n. you feel sure about your abilities, qualities, or ideas 信心 U9P1
conflict [ˈkɒnflɪkt] n. a situation in which people, groups or countries are involved in a serious disagreement or argument 冲突, 争执 U10P3B
conjunctivitis [kənˌdʒʌŋktɪˈvaɪtɪs] n. a disease that causes swelling in the eye 结膜炎 U3P3B
connection [kəˈnekʃn] n. something that connects two facts, ideas, etc. （两种事实、观念等的）联系, 关联 U10P3B
constantly [ˈkɒnstəntli] adv. all the time; repeatedly 始终, 一直 U10P3A
contaminate [kənˈtæmɪneɪt] v. to make a substance or place dirty or no longer pure by adding something that is dangerous or carries disease 污染, 弄脏 U10P3A
contend [kənˈtend] v. to compete against someone to gain something 竞争, 争夺 U7P3B
coronary [ˈkɒrən(ə)rɪ] adj. the blood vessels surrounding the heart 冠状动脉或静脉的 U4P3B
coronavirus [kəˌrəʊnəˈvaɪərəs] n. a type of airborne virus 冠状病毒 U5P3A
corrector [kəˈrektə] n. someone or something to make something right or accurate 修正者 U10P3A
cross [krɒs] v. beyond a limit or boundary 超过, 超出 U7P3A
cuisine [kwɪˈziːn] n. a style of cooking 烹饪 U7P3A

calm...down (使)平静下来；(使)镇定下来　　　　　　　　　　　　　　　　　　U9P3B
check off 逐一核对　　　　　　　　　　　　　　　　　　　　　　　　　　　U7P3B
compare to 与……相比　　　　　　　　　　　　　　　　　　　　　　　　　U5P3A
cover up 遮盖，掩饰　　　　　　　　　　　　　　　　　　　　　　　　　　U3P3B

D

decay [dɪˈkeɪ] v. to be destroyed gradually by natural processes 腐烂，腐朽　　U3P3B
delicacy [ˈdelɪkəsɪ] n. a kind of food considered to be very nice to eat 美味佳肴　U7P3A
demonstrate [ˈdemənstreɪt] v. to establish the validity of something 证明，表明　U2P3B
deodorant [diːˈəʊdərənt] n. a substance that people prevent unpleasant smells 除味剂　U3P3B
depression [dɪˈpreʃn] n. a mental state in which you are sad and feel that you cannot enjoy anything, because your situation is so difficult and unpleasant 沮丧　　U9P1
depressive [dɪˈpresɪv] adj. connected with the medical condition of depression 抑郁的　U1P3A
detection [dɪˈtekʃ(ə)n] n. the perception that something has occurred 侦查，察觉　U4P3B
device [dɪˈvaɪs] n. an instrument invented for a particular purpose 装置　　　　U4P3B
diary [ˈdaɪərɪ] n. a daily written record of (usually personal) experiences and observations 日记
　　　　　　　　　　　　　　　　　　　　　　　　　　　　　　　　　　　U5P3B
disperse [dɪˈspɜːs] v. to move apart and go away in different directions; to make somebody/something do this 驱散，分散　　　　　　　　　　　　　　　　　　　　　　　U5P3B
distribute [dɪˈstrɪbjuːt] v. to spread widely 分布，散布　　　　　　　　　　　U2P3A
documentary [ˌdɒkjʊˈmentrɪ] n. television or radio programmes, or films, recording facts about something 纪录片　　　　　　　　　　　　　　　　　　　　　　　　U7P3A
domestic [dəˈmestɪk] adj. of or inside a particular country; not foreign or international 本国的，国内的　　　　　　　　　　　　　　　　　　　　　　　　　　　　　　　U8P3B
dorm [dɔːm] n. a room for several people to sleep in, esp. in an institution 集体宿舍，学生宿舍
　　　　　　　　　　　　　　　　　　　　　　　　　　　　　　　　　　　U1P1
dramatically [drəˈmætɪklɪ] adv. a dramatic change or event happens suddenly and is very noticeable and surprising 突如其来地，急剧地　　　　　　　　　　　　　　　U5P3A

date back 追溯　　　　　　　　　　　　　　　　　　　　　　　　　　　　　U2P3A
deal with 处理，应付　　　　　　　　　　　　　　　　　　　　　　　　　　U7P3B
divert...away from 从……转移　　　　　　　　　　　　　　　　　　　　　　U9P3B
dozens of 几十　　　　　　　　　　　　　　　　　　　　　　　　　　　　　U7P3A

E

eatery [ˈiːtərɪ] n. restaurants or other places serving food 餐馆，饭店　　　　　U7P3A
embrace [ɪmˈbreɪs] v. to accept an idea, a proposal, a set of beliefs, etc., especially when it is done with enthusiasm 欣然接受，乐意采纳　　　　　　　　　　　　　　　U1P3B
emotion [ɪˈməʊʃn] n. a feeling such as happiness, love, fear, anger, or hatred, which can be caused by the situation that you are in or the people you are with 情感　　　　U9P1
employ [ɪmˈplɔɪ] v. to give somebody a job to do for payment 雇用　　　　　　U5P3A
endorphin [enˈdɔːfɪn] n. a chemical naturally released in the brain to reduce pain 内啡肽　U9P3A
enhance [ɪnˈhɑːns] v. to raise the level of something 提升　　　　　　　　　　U2P3B
event [ɪˈvent] n. a thing that happens, especially something important 事件，大事　U6P3B

Glossary

eventually [ɪˈventʃuəli] adv. at the end of a period of time or a series of events 最后，最终 U5P3B
evolutionary [ˌiːvəˈluːʃənəri] adj. relating to evolution or development 进化的 U2P3A
evolve [ɪˈvɒlv] v. work out 发展，进化，使逐步形成 U4P3B
excessively [ɪkˈsesɪvli] adv. to a degree exceeding normal or proper limits 过分地，极度地 U1P3A
exfoliate [eksˈfəʊlieɪt] v. to remove dead cells from the surface of skin 使死皮脱落 U3P3B
expand [ɪkˈspænd] v. become larger in size or volume or quantity 扩大，增大 U1P3B
expertise [ˌekspɜːˈtiːz] n. expert knowledge or skill in a particular subject, activity or job 专门知识，专门技能，专长 U8P3B
exposure [ɪkˈspəʊʒə] n. when someone experiences something or is affected by it because he or she is in a particular situation or place 暴露，曝光 U4P3A

even if 即使 U9P3A

F

fascinate [ˈfæsɪneɪt] v. to attract or interest somebody very much 使着迷，使神魂颠倒 U8P3A
feature [ˈfiːtʃə] n. qualities or characteristics 特点，特征 U2P3A
fencing [ˈfensɪŋ] n. the sport of fighting with long thin swords 击剑 U6P1
fetus [ˈfiːtəs] n. an unborn or unhatched vertebrate in the later stages of development showing the main recognizable features of the mature animal 胎，胎儿 U10P1
financial [faɪˈnænʃl] adj. connected with money and finance 财政的，金融的 U10P3A
finger [ˈfɪŋɡə(r)] n. one of the four long thin parts that stick out from the hand (or five, if the thumb is included) 手指 U3P1
fingertip [ˈfɪŋətɪp] n. the end of the finger that is the furthest from the hand 指尖 U1P3B
Finnish [ˈfɪnɪʃ] n. belonging or relating to Finland or to its people, language, or culture 芬兰的，芬兰人的 U5P3A
follicle [ˈfɒlɪkl] n. the small holes in the skin, especially one that a hair grows from (毛)囊 U5P3B
foodstuff [ˈfuːdstʌf] n. any substance that is used as food 食物，食品 U8P1
futuristic [ˌfjuːtʃəˈrɪstɪk] adj. extremely modern and unusual, as if coming from the future 极具现代的，未来派的 U7P3A

figure out 弄明白，想出 U7P3B
first race 第一名 U6P3B
flight of stairs 阶梯 U6P3B
focus on 使……聚焦 U9P3A
food labeling 食品标签 U4P3A
the five rings of Olympics 奥运五环 U6P3B

G

gem [dʒem] n. a precious stone that has been cut and polished and is used in jewelry 宝石，珍宝 U7P3A
generic [dʒɪˈnerɪk] adj. (of a product, especially a drug) not using the name of the company that made it 无厂家商标的，非专利的 U8P3B
genuine [ˈdʒenjuɪn] adj. to describe people and things that are exactly what they appear to be, and

are not false or an imitation 真正的，非伪造的，名副其实的 　　　　　　　　　　　　U8P3B

geographical [ˌdʒɪəˈɡræfɪkl] adj. relating to the study of the earth's surface 地理学的　　U7P3A

geothermal [ˌdʒiːəʊˈθɜːml] adj. relating to the heat in the interior of the earth 地热的　　U7P3A

globe [ɡləʊb] n. the world (used especially to emphasize its size) 地球，世界　　　　U10P3A

guarantee [ˌɡærənˈtiː] v. something that is a guarantee of something else makes it certain that it will happen or that it is true 保证　　　　　　　　　　　　　　　　　　　　　U8P3B

guardian [ˈɡɑːdɪən] n. a person who is legally responsible for the care of another person, especially a child whose parents have died 监护人　　　　　　　　　　　　　　U1P3A

gym [dʒɪm] n. a room or hall with equipment for doing physical exercises, for example in a school 体育馆　　　　　　　　　　　　　　　　　　　　　　　　　　　　U1P1

gymnastics [dʒɪmˈnæstɪks] n. physical exercises that develop and show the body's strength and ability to move and bend easily 体操　　　　　　　　　　　　　　　　　U6P1

get into...habits 养成……的习惯　　　　　　　　　　　　　　　　　　U3P3B

go after 追求　　　　　　　　　　　　　　　　　　　　　　　　　U10P3B

go through 通过　　　　　　　　　　　　　　　　　　　　　　　　U10P3B

H

harmless [ˈhɑːmlɪs] adj. not causing or capable of causing harm 无害的，不致伤的　　U4P3A

harmony [ˈhɑːməni] n. the state of constancy in opinion or action 和谐　　　　U2P3A

headboard [ˈhedbɔːd] n. the vertical board at the end of a bed 床头板　　　　U5P3B

heaven [ˈhevn] n. the place believed to be the home of God where good people go when they die 天堂，天国　　　　　　　　　　　　　　　　　　　　　　　　　U5P3B

hold [həʊld] v. to carry something; to have somebody/something in your hands, arms, etc. 拿住，握住　　　　　　　　　　　　　　　　　　　　　　　　　U6P3A

honor [ˈɒnə(r)] v. bestow honor or rewards upon 给予荣誉　　　　　　　U6P3B

hormone [ˈhɔːməʊn] n. a chemical substance produced in the body or in a plant that encourages growth or influences how the cells and tissues function 激素　　　　　U1P3A

have tremendous impacts on 对……产生巨大影响　　　　　　　　　　U1P3A

heart-burning 不满　　　　　　　　　　　　　　　　　　　　　　　U10P3B

host country 东道国　　　　　　　　　　　　　　　　　　　　　　U6P3A

I

immune [ɪˈmjuːn] adj. cannot catch or be affected by a particular disease 免疫的　U3P3A

immunologist [ˌɪmjʊˈnɒlədʒɪst] n. a medical scientist who specializes in immunology 免疫学专家　　　　　　　　　　　　　　　　　　　　　　　　　　　　U3P3A

implementation [ˌɪmplɪmenˈteɪʃn] n. the act of accomplishing some aim or executing some order 实施　　　　　　　　　　　　　　　　　　　　　　　　　　　U8P3B

impressive [ɪmˈpresɪv] adj. making a strong or vivid impression 给人印象深刻的　U5P3A

incredible [ɪnˈkredəbl] adj. extremely good 极好的，了不起的　　　　　U7P3B

indicate [ˈɪndɪkeɪt] v. to show or suggest 指出，表明　　　　　　　　U2P3B

indispensable [ˌɪndɪsˈpensəbl] adj. too important to be without 不可或缺的，必不可少的　U8P3A

induce [ɪnˈdjuːs] v. cause to arise 引诱　　　　　　　　　　　　　　U2P3A

infant [ˈɪnfənt] n. a baby or very young child 婴儿，幼儿　　U10P1
infect [ɪnˈfekt] v. to make a disease spread to a person or a plant 感染　　U3P3B
infection [ɪnˈfekʃn] n. the act or process of causing or getting a disease 感染　　U3P3B
inner [ˈɪnə(r)] adj. the parts contained or enclosed inside the other parts, closest to the center 内心的　　U9P3A
inspire [ɪnˈspaɪə] v. to encourage or stimulate someone 鼓励　　U2P3B
instrument [ˈɪnstrəmənt] n. a musical device that requires skill for proper use 乐器　　U2P1
interrupt [ˌɪntəˈrʌpt] v. to stop something for a short time 使暂停，使中断　　U6P3A
involve [ɪnˈvɒlv] v. to engage as a participant 包含，牵涉　　U2P3A
irregular [ɪˈreɡjʊlə(r)] adj. occurring at uneven or varying rates or intervals 不规则的　　U9P3B
irritation [ˌɪrɪˈteɪʃn] n. a feeling of slight pain and discomfort 刺激，疼痛　　U3P3B
isolate [ˈaɪsəleɪt] v. place or set apart 使隔离，使孤立　　U4P3B

immerse in 沉浸在……　　U1P3B
immune system 免疫系统　　U4P3A
in instant 立刻　　U10P3B
in the midst of 当某是发生时，处于……中　　U10P3B

K
kitchen [ˈkɪtʃɪn] n. a room in which meals are cooked or prepared 厨房　　U5P1

keep away from 远离，回避　　U3P3A
keep... in check 控制　　U10P3A

L
lab [læb] n. a room or building used for scientific research, experiments, testing, etc. 实验室　　U1P1
library [ˈlaɪbrəri] n. a building in which collections of books, CDs, newspapers, etc. are kept for people to read, study or borrow 图书馆　　U1P1
luggage [ˈlʌɡɪdʒ] n. cases, bags, etc. that contain people's things when they are traveling 行李　　U7P1
lycopene [ˈlaɪkəpiːn] n. carotenoid that makes tomatoes red 番茄红素　　U4P3B
lyric [ˈlɪrɪk] n. the text of a song 歌词　　U2P1

lead to 导致，通向　　U3P3B
lean into 倾向　　U10P3B
lighten up 放轻松，开心一些　　U10P3B

M
mandate [ˈmændeɪt] v. to order somebody to behave or do something in a particular way 强制执行，委托办理　　U5P3A
manufacture [ˌmænjʊˈfæktʃə(r)] v. to make goods in large quantities, using machinery 大量生产，成批制造　　U10P3A
massive [ˈmæsɪv] adj. very large in size 非常大的　　U9P3B

135

medication [ˌmedɪˈkeɪʃn] n. a drug or another form of medicine that you take to prevent or to treat an illness 药品 　　　　　　　　　　　　　　　　　　　　　　　　　　U8P1

memory [ˈmeməri] n. a thought of something that you remember from the past 回忆　　U5P3B

mental [ˈmentl] adj. relating to the state or the health of a person's mind 心理的　　U9P1

mentally [ˈmentəli] adv. in your mind 心理上　　　　　　　　　　　　　　　　　U9P3A

mentor [ˈmentɔːr] v. to give someone help and advice over a period of time, especially help and advice related to their job 指导，辅导　　　　　　　　　　　　　　　　　　U1P3B

metropolis [mɪˈtrɒpəlɪs] n. a large important city in a country or region 大都会，大城市　　U7P3A

microbe [ˈmaɪkrəʊb] n. a minute life form (especially a disease-causing bacterium) 微生物，细菌
　　　　　　　　　　　　　　　　　　　　　　　　　　　　　　　　　　　U4P3A

minimize [ˈmɪnɪmaɪz] v. to reduce something, especially something bad to the lowest possible level 使减少到最低限度　　　　　　　　　　　　　　　　　　　　　　　　U1P3A

misfortune [mɪsˈfɔːtʃʊn] n. something unpleasant or unlucky that happens to someone 不幸，厄运
　　　　　　　　　　　　　　　　　　　　　　　　　　　　　　　　　　　U5P3B

motivate [ˈməʊtɪveɪt] v. give an incentive for action 激发……的积极性　　　　　　　U9P3B

multiple [ˈmʌltɪpl] adj. having or involving or consisting of more than one part 多样的，许多的
　　　　　　　　　　　　　　　　　　　　　　　　　　　　　　　　　　　U8P3A

municipality [mjuːˌnɪsɪˈpælətɪ] n. a city, town or district with its own government 自治市，直辖市
　　　　　　　　　　　　　　　　　　　　　　　　　　　　　　　　　　　U7P3A

muscle [ˈmʌsl] n. a piece of tissue inside your body that connects two bones and that you use when you make a movement 肌肉　　　　　　　　　　　　　　　　　　　　U9P3B

N

necessity [nəˈsesəti] n. a thing that you must have in order to live properly or do something 必需品　　　　　　　　　　　　　　　　　　　　　　　　　　　　　　　　U8P1

negative [ˈnegətɪv] adj. unpleasant, depressing, or harmful 消极的　　　　　　　U9P1

neglect [nɪˈglekt] v. to not give enough attention to something 忽视，不予重视　　U10P3A

neural [ˈnjʊərəl] adj. regarding the nervous system 神经的　　　　　　　　　　U2P3A

nobleman [ˈnəʊblmən] n. a man who was a member of the nobility (男)贵族　　　U3P3A

noodle [ˈnuːd(ə)l] n. a ribbonlike strip of pasta 面条　　　　　　　　　　　　U4P1

notion [ˈnəʊʃ(ə)n] n. a general inclusive idea 概念，观念　　　　　　　　　　U2P3B

nutrient [ˈnjuːtrɪənt] n. a substance that is needed to keep a living thing alive and to help it to grow 养分，营养物　　　　　　　　　　　　　　　　　　　　　　　　　U10P3A

O

obesity [ə(ʊ)ˈbiːsəti] n. more than average fatness 肥胖，肥胖症　　　　　　　U4P3B

occupation [ˌɒkjʊˈpeɪʃn] n. a job or profession 工作，职业　　　　　　　　　U10P3A

odour [ˈəʊdə(r)] n. a smell, especially one that is unpleasant 臭味　　　　　　U3P3B

Olympic [əˈlɪmpɪk] adj. relating to the Olympic Games 奥林匹克的　　　　　　U6P3A

organism [ˈɔːgənɪzəm] n. a living thing that has the ability to act independently 有机物　U2P3A

overall [ˌəʊvərˈɔːl] adv. generally; when you consider everything 一般来说，大体上　U5P3A

Ohio State University 俄亥俄州立大学　　　　　　　　　　　　　　　　　U6P3B

on the average 平均而言　　　　　　　　　　　　　　　　　　　　　　U5P3A

136

on the other hand 另一方面 U4P3B

on track 在正道上，未离题（或目标），正轨 U9P3A

P

palm [pɑːm] n. the inner surface of the hand between the wrist and fingers 手掌 U3P1

pandemic [pæn'demɪk] n. a disease that spreads over a whole country or the whole world （全国或全球性）流行病，大流行病 U10P3A

panic ['pænɪk] n. a very strong feeling of anxiety or fear that makes you act without thinking carefully 恐慌 U9P3B

particularly [pə'tɪkjʊləlɪ] adv. to a distinctly greater extent or degree than common 特别地，独特地 U4P3A

peak [piːk] adj. used to describe the highest level of something, or a time when the greatest number of people are doing something or using something 高峰的，高峰期的 U7P3B

permit [pə'mɪt] n. an official document which gives someone the right to do something 许可证，特许证 U7P3B

perspective [pə'spektɪv] n. an idea of thinking about something 观点 U9P3A

phytochemical [faɪtəʊ'kemɪk(ə)l] adj. 植物化学的 U4P3B

pilot ['paɪlət] adj. a pilot plan or a pilot project is one that is used to test an idea before deciding whether to introduce it on a larger scale 试验性的 U8P3A

platform ['plætfɔːm] n. the combination of a particular computer and a particular operating system 平台 U8P3A

political [pə'lɪtɪkl] adj. connected with the state, government or public affairs 政治的 U6P3B

portion ['pɔːʃn] n. an amount of food that is large enough for a person （食物）一份 U1P3A

positive ['pɒzətɪv] adj. hopeful and confident, thinking of the good aspects of a situation rather than the bad ones 积极的 U9P1

potential [pə'tenʃl] n. the necessary abilities or qualities to become successful or useful in the future 潜力，潜能 U9P3A

practically ['præktɪklɪ] adv. almost; very nearly 几乎，差不多 U10P3B

prayer [preər] n. words which you say to God giving thanks or asking for help 祈祷 U5P3B

precious ['preʃəs] adj. rare and worth a lot of money 珍奇的，珍稀的 U10P3A

preschooler ['priːˈskuːlə(r)] n. children who are no longer babies but are not yet old enough to go to school 学龄前儿童 U10P1

priority [praɪ'ɒrətɪ] n. something that you think is more important than other things and should be dealt with first 优先事项，最重要的事 U7P3B

prostate ['prɒsteɪt] n. a firm partly muscular chestnut sized gland in males at the neck of the urethra 前列腺 U4P3B

psychologist [saɪ'kɒlədʒɪst] n. the professional specializing in psychology 心理学家 U2P3B

puberty ['pjuːbətɪ] n. when the body starts to become mature 青春期 U3P3B

publish ['pʌblɪʃ] v. to produce a book, magazine, CD-ROM, etc., and sell it to the public 出版，发行 U6P3A

purposefully ['pɜːpəsfʊlɪ] adv. in a purposeful manner 有意地 U1P3A

push [pʊʃ] v. to use your hands, arms or body in order to make somebody/something move forward or away from you; to move part of your body into a particular position 推动（人或物） U10P3B

part-time 兼职工作 U6P3B
pass on to 传递给…… U5P3B
physical togetherness 现实生活中的团聚 U5P3A
practice social distancing 保持社交距离 U5P3A
prevent from 阻止，防止 U9P3B

Q

quote [kwəʊt] n. a punctuation mark used to attribute the enclosed text to someone else 引文，引语 U10P3B

quell one's anxiety 消除某人的焦虑 U1P3A

R

racial [ˈreɪʃl] adj. happening or existing between people of different races 种族的，种族间的 U5P3B

raise [reɪz] v. to increase the amount or level of something 增加 U6P3A

ranger [ˈreɪndʒə(r)] n. a person who takes care of a forest, a park or an area of countryside 护林员 U7P3B

recognize [ˈrekəgnaɪz] v. to know who somebody is or what something is when you see or hear them, because you have seen or heard them before 认识，辨别出 U5P3B

refer [rɪˈfɜː(r)] v. to mention or speak about someone or something 提到，谈及 U7P3A

refinish [riːˈfɪnɪʃ] v. give a new surface 再抛光，修整表面 U5P3B

refuse [rɪˈfjuːz] v. to say that you will not do something that somebody has asked you to do 拒绝 U6P3B

regard [rɪˈɡɑːd] v. to think about somebody/something in a particular way 认为，视为 U6P3B

registration [ˌredʒɪˈstreɪʃn] n. the act of enrolling 注册 U8P3A

reinforce [ˌriːɪnˈfɔːs] v. make stronger or more intense 加强 U9P3A

relationship [rɪˈleɪʃnʃɪp] n. the way in which two people, groups or countries behave towards each other or deal with each other 关系，联系 U10P3B

religion [rɪˈlɪdʒən] n. the belief in the existence of a god or gods, and the activities that are connected with the worship of them 宗教，宗教信仰 U5P3B

remarkably [rɪˈmɑːkəbli] adv. to a remarkable degree or extent 非常，显著地，格外 U5P3A

reminder [rɪˈmaɪndə(r)] n. something that makes you think about or remember somebody/something, that you have forgotten or would like to forget 引起回忆的事，提醒人的事 U10P3A

remove [rɪˈmuːv] v. to take somebody or something away from a place 移开，去掉 U3P3A

replace [rɪˈpleɪs] v. to be used instead of somebody/something else; to do something instead of somebody/something else 代替，取代 U10P3B

reply [rɪˈplaɪ] v. to say or write something as an answer to somebody/something 回答，答复 U6P3B

resilience [rɪˈzɪliəns] n. the ability to recover quickly from difficulties; toughness 恢复力 U9P3A

restriction [rɪˈstrɪkʃn] n. a principle that limits the extent of something 限制，约束 U4P3A

restroom [ˈrestruːm] n. a room with a toilet in a public place, such as a theatre or a restaurant 洗手间，盥洗室 U5P1

resume [rɪˈzjuːm] v. if you resume an activity or if it resumes, it begins again 重新开始 U6P3A

Glossary

rhythm [ˈrɪð(ə)m] n. recurring at regular intervals in music 节奏 U2P1

routine [ruːˈtiːn] n. the normal way in which you regularly do things 常规,惯例 U3P3B

rule [ruːl] n. a statement of what may, must or must not be done in a particular situation or when playing a game 规则,规章 U6P3A

reflection 反应 U10P3A

regardless of 不管 U10P3A

release a message 发布消息 U10P3A

rely on 依靠,依赖 U4P3B

remind...of 提醒 U10P3A

S

sadden [ˈsædn] v. to make somebody sad 使悲伤,使伤心 U1P3A

sand [sænd] v. to make something smooth by rubbing it with sandpaper or a sander 用砂纸打磨 U5P3B

schedule [ˈʃedjuːl] n. a plan that lists all the work that you have to do and when you must do them 日程安排 U7P3B

scholarship [ˈskɒləʃɪp] n. an amount of money given to somebody by an organization to help pay for their education 奖学金 U1P3B

scientifically [ˌsaɪənˈtɪfɪklɪ] adv. involving science 科学地 U3P3A

scratch [skrætʃ] n. a mark, a cut or an injury made by scratching somebody's skin or the surface of something 划痕,划伤 U5P3B

semantic [sɪˈmæntɪk] adj. relating to meaning 语义的 U2P3B

sense [sens] v. to become aware of something even though you cannot see it, hear it, etc. 感觉到,意识到 U5P3B

shiny [ˈʃaɪnɪ] adj. smooth and bright; reflecting the light 光亮的,锃亮的 U3P3A

signal [ˈsɪgnəl] n. a sound or movement made to give someone information or instructions 信号 U7P3B

skip [skɪp] v. to leave out something 遗漏,略过 U7P3B

skyscraper [ˈskaɪˌskreɪpə(r)] n. very tall modern buildings in a city 摩天楼 U7P3A

slave [sleɪv] n. someone who is the property of another person and has to work for that person 奴隶 U6P3B

snack [snæk] n. a light informal meal 小吃,快餐 U4P3B

soap [səʊp] n. a substance that you use with water for washing your body 肥皂 U3P1

soccer [ˈsɒkə(r)] n. a game in which two teams of eleven players try to kick or head a ball into the opponents' goal 足球 U6P1

sociable [ˈsəʊʃəbl] adj. enjoying spending time with other people 好交际的,合群的 U1P3A

sole [səʊl] n. the bottom surface of the foot 脚掌,脚底(板) U3P3B

sophomore [ˈsɒfəmɔːr] n. a student in the second year of a college or university (大学)二年级学生 U1P3B

souvenir [ˌsuːvəˈnɪər] n. a thing that you buy and/or keep to remind yourself of a place, an occasion or a holiday/vacation 纪念品,纪念物 U1P3A

spicy [ˈspaɪsɪ] adj. food having a strong taste with spices in it 辛辣的 U7P3A

sportsman [ˈspɔːtsmən] n. a person who takes part in sport, especially someone who is very good at it 运动员 U6P3A

sportswear [ˈspɔːtsweə(r)] n. clothes that are worn for playing sports, or in informal situations 运动服装 U6P3A

spot [spɒt] v. to see or notice a person or thing, especially suddenly 发现，认出 U7P3B

stage [steɪdʒ] n. the structure for varieties of art performances 舞台 U2P1

stale [steɪl] adj. lacking originality or spontaneity; no longer new 陈腐的 U10P3B

stamp [stæmp] n. a small piece of paper with a design on it that you buy and stick on an envelope or a package before you post it 邮票，标志 U6P3A

steam [stiːm] v. cook food with the hot gas produced when water boils 蒸 U4P1

stimulation [ˌstɪmjʊˈleɪʃn] n. the act of stimulating 刺激 U2P3A

stimulus [ˈstɪmjʊləs] n. something which may speed up decisions 刺激 U2P3A

strengthen [ˈstreŋθn] v. to become stronger; to make somebody/something stronger 加强，增强 U10P3A

stress [stres] n. you feel worried and tense because of difficulties in your life 压力 U9P1

striker [ˈstraɪkə(r)] n. a worker who has stopped working because of a disagreement over pay or conditions 罢工者 U5P3B

strip [strɪp] v. to remove all the things from a place and leave it empty 拆除 U5P3B

stuffed [stʌft] adj. filled with something 已经喂饱了的，塞满了的 U4P1

sufficient [səˈfɪʃnt] adj. enough for a particular purpose; as much as you need 足够的，充足的 U1P3A

surround [səˈraʊnd] v. to be all around something or somebody 围绕，环绕 U1P3B

survival [səˈvaɪvl] n. remaining alive 幸存 U2P3A

swimming [ˈswɪmɪŋ] n. the activity of swimming, especially as a sport or for pleasure 游泳，游泳运动 U6P1

symptom [ˈsɪmptəm] n. something wrong with your body or mind that is a sign of the illness 症状 U9P3B

second-year student 大二年级学生 U6P3B
see...as 把……看作 U10P3A
senior citizen 老年人 U10P1
stop the growth 停止增长 U4P3B

T

temptation [tempˈteɪʃn] n. the desire to do or have something that you know is bad or wrong 引诱，诱惑 U1P3A

threatened [ˈθretənd] adj. feel as if you are in danger 受到威胁的 U7P3B

toddler [ˈtɒdlə(r)] n. a young child who has only just learned to walk or who still walks unsteadily with small, quick steps 蹒跚行走的人，学步的幼儿 U10P1

togetherness [təˈgeðərnɪs] n. the happy feeling you have when you are with people you like, especially family and friends （尤指家庭或朋友的）和睦相处，亲密无间 U5P3A

track [træk] v. to find somebody/something by following the marks, signs, information, etc. that they have left behind them 跟踪，追踪 U10P3B

trail [treɪl] n. a route that is followed for a particular purpose 路线，路径 U7P3B

transition [trænˈzɪʃn] n. the process or a period of changing from one state or condition to

Glossary

another 过渡,变迁,转变 U1P3B

thanks to 由于 U7P3A
tend to 倾向于 U7P3A
turn out 结果是 U10P3B

U

urge [ɜːdʒ] v. to advise or try hard to persuade someone to do something 敦促,催促 U5P3A

under the same roof 在同一屋檐下,同处一室 U5P3A
unimpeded **trade policy** 自由贸易政策 U8P3A

V

vehicle [ˈviːɪkl] n. things that are used to carry people or goods from one place to another, such as a car or a bus 交通工具 U7P1
volleyball [ˈvɒlibɔːl] n. a game in which two teams of six players use their hands to hit a large ball backwards and forwards over a high net while trying not to let the ball touch the ground on their own side 排球 U6P1

W

weather [ˈweðə(r)] n. the condition of the atmosphere at a particular place and time 天气 U7P1
wedding [ˈwedɪŋ] n. a marriage ceremony, and the meal or party that usually follows it a wedding present 婚礼,结婚庆典 U5P3B
witness [ˈwɪtnɪs] v. to perceive or be contemporaneous with 见证,目击 U8P3A
wrist [rɪst] n. a joint between the hand and the arm 手腕 U3P1

wash away 冲走,清洗,消除 U3P3A
wealth of 大量的,丰富的 U7P3B
White Olympic 白色奥运会 U6P3A
with the implementation of 随着……的实施 U8P3A

注:单词出处 U1P3B 的意思为 Unit 1 Part 3 Passage B,其他类推;斜写体单词为超出高等学校英语应用能力考试(PRETCO)大纲的词汇。